A Bee in Monet's Garden

Lyrical Prose

Jean-Yves Vincent Ciccariello Solinga

Leaning Rock Press
Gales Ferry, CT

Leaning Rock Press
Gales Ferry, CT 06335
leaningrockpress@gmail.com
www.leaningrockpress.com

978-1-960596-48-2, Hardcover
978-1-960596-49-9, Softcover

Cover: Painting by Claude Monet, 'Prunieurs en fleurs', 1879 (Public Domain)

Library of Congress Control Number: 2024920507

Publisher's Cataloging-in-Publication
(Provided by Cassidy Cataloguing Services, Inc.)

Names:	Solinga, Jean-Yves, author.
Title:	A bee in Monet's Garden : lyrical prose / Jean-Yves Vincent Ciccariello Solinga.
Description:	Gales Ferry, CT : Leaning Rock Press, [2024]
Identifiers:	ISBN: 978-1-960596-48-2 (hardcover)	978-1-960596-49-9 (softcover)	LCCN: 024920507
Subjects:	LCSH: Reality--Poetry.	Existentialism--Poetry.	Absurd (Philosophy)--Poetry.	Aesthetics-- Poetry.	Space and time--Poetry.	LCGFT: Poetry.	BISAC: POETRY / General.
Classification:	LCC: PS3619.O4326 B44 2024	DDC: 811/.6--dc23

Printed in the United States of America

Dedication

To my parents:
Whose new-world visions, I hope, I have seeded well.

Acknowledgment

To my wife, Elaine:
For her love and support.

Contents

Preface

It was not on the scale of a biblical event, but the death of my 'boyhood Rooster' giving up his body, for a life-altering 'last' couscous, became one the many metaphors that have energized my writing. Whether intimate terrasse-café, conversations amid Paris traffic; Floral perfumes from Grasse; emanating from body heat or a freshly baked baguette. Even the 'emptiness' of the Magrheban Bled: [à la Led Zeppelin's Kashmir] ... filled my being with a solar presence. The rich complexity and nuances of moments: of the venerated hotel, bedroom-walls, of Saint-Germain-des-Prés. 'Moments within moments'... to be shared with the 'other': the way prehistoric tribes felt a need to share the beauty of the outside fauna; depicted in shades of colored mud on the wall of their grottoes.

The basic creative drive has not changed much.

In my case, it all seems to have begun, on that cold winter-night of my teenage years: rolling around... intertwined on ice and snow: in a vacant field. Then, rushing home: to my 'new world' miserable bedroom... but also having the budding instinctive passion and creative reflex, to write it down, on sheets of 'college-rule-lined paper'.

And like that intoxicated bee... extracting lyrical moments from the various bits of a life; into what would become the organically ethereal material of a reconstructed past [with none of the inert, artificial codes of A.I] but rather the fruitful relationship between the cerebral, yet sensual... human... written thoughts. Thus, turning the miserable conditions of the "... emptiness of this frozen, New England field, into the timeless shorthand of the metaphor. In this iconic situation, a teenage rite of passage, in a muddy and puzzling culture. Leaving [HER] behind in this emotional [American] landscape of moral disjunction, abuse and ambient violence. The artist, feeling guilty of using the privilege and protective patina of semi-fiction that allow artists to use fragments of reality, for their arbitrary literary needs.

1

Thus, enters "Barka: the fictionalized concept". Versus: Barka the local Berber; young woman; who became a mother's helper and thus the image of "Maman Barka".

Barka: the poem

She had lain in an old briefcase:
On the top shelf, behind unused cookbooks.

Captured in a black and white photo.
The intensity of the Maghreban sun: still the main character.

A side comment, about the Moroccan-cumin in last night's dish,
followed by a visceral synesthesia:
reconstructing the smell of fresh "khubz" or "ksra" bread
from the souk of his youth.

———

She is back…
… her vaporous curves, selfishly hiding behind the white, pudic,
cotton-screen of a flowing summer djellaba…
… his pubescent glance…
trying to interpret the language of this doubly, strange universe.

As though in magical unison:
The duality of the dangerous attraction of the engorged crimson prickly
pears, scented their moment.

Near Sidi Moussa,**
in the rocky privacy of a cave overlooking a minuscule beach:
beyond all social and religious commandments,
joyfully ignoring conventions:

Youth did, what it does best:
Create the privacy of time-warps, where dreams help escape reality.

Far... far away from the artifice of smart technologies.
or the mind-numbing, servile equations of mathematics...
... THE EXPANSE OF THE UNIVERSE
allowed itself to be held in their grasp:
IT...
could, indeed, be tamed, appeased... by the simple stroke of fingers tips.
The closing of eye lids, upon a kiss.

————

That hot afternoon
-with the green Atlantic and the yellow bled as witnesses-
their untouched flesh would be properly sacrificed on nature's altar.

Not with ceremonial of incantations.
Not with burning incent.
Not with imposed oaths:

But rather through life-giving, organic sighs.
Youthful offerings on the tabernacle to Mediterranean gods:
Humanity's carnal eternity.

————

From shards, chiseled in Grecian marble:
the one reserved for its divinities.

From uncontrollable outbursts.
Like escaped spirits from the soul:
found in the gentle afternoon darkness of curtains.

Like a "Last Tango in Paris".
Like a priceless statuette, nervously broken on a Parisian parquet floor.
Like beads of salty sweat mindlessly tasted.

Like a quick, last glance toward her climbing into a taxi.
Like envying the coffee rim, caressed by her blood-red lips...

And still... and always.
The artist's... any artist's... recurrent fear:
The need to fill the present... with pieces of its past.

Had Barka… and others like her…
stopped to exist after the shutter's closing?

Had she not fully reappeared in that tiny black and white photograph?
What of the similar Others?
What part of them had been fictions of reality?

There is, in art and the artist, an insatiable, creative abyss:
to be filled by the only currency capable of capturing time:

Our lawless, cosmologically untethered,
human… sentient consciousness.

————

Having bounced images of his muse
off the walls of the tiny Parisian hotel:
He reconstructed her.

Like a little boy, breaking his new watch:
"To see where time comes from".
The artist takes apart pieces of moments, to reconstruct its elements:
helping sooth the longing of icons of happiness.

Having left Barka… as he looked at her receding image
in the oval of the rear of the Volkswagen,
he would honor their nuptials and
their continuing existence
through the fiction of their love.

————

… they had not seen each other since youth:
but reality only controls the minerals of asteroids.
And, occasionally,
the universe liberates parts of itself.

There can, therefore,
exist poetry
in the freedom of cosmic randomness.

Barka… never did leave him after that afternoon.
The cold atoms… themselves,
in a gigantic divine dispensation, had insulated these two lives
from the imposition of linear time.

Her glance… full of the hazel reflections of the symbolic richness of her
Berber blood, ***
… had been the last thing he remembered before…
making one out of two.

** *Sidi Moussa, near Salé: family fishing promontory, overlooking the Atlantic Ocean.*

*** *Roman soldiers from northern Europe.*

———————

Author's marginal notes:

Re-rereading my notes and pivotal poems; full of excruciating rawness, excavating into the rich and deep dirt of undisclosed… and or… undisclosable knowledge of confessional moments [to and by] the author/writer's voice], this poem… this figure… this setting… became spontaneously a curtain of modesty to explore the author-text… reality-fiction relationship: in all my work. And of course, returning regularly to my notes on Roland Barthes.

———————

This person of… and in my youth… (and left in my youth) reconstituted herself: as though having come in contact with the proper liquid: to add to the lifeless powder of the past. For my purpose, I will call her "Barka". The same as the real person in my past. I like whom she was and is to me. I like the sound; I like how I had to reconstruct her from family pictures and souvenirs. This is exactly what Poland Barthes liked in his analysis if the "death of the author": in other words: who is… and what is this author? And what is his or her relationship to the artistic "creation". "Barka" would become the exact foil for how my poetry developed itself. She was somehow like anti-matter; I could lose myself in my creation. Her description could be dictated "by her"! her presence in my text could be be "radio-active": not "her" per say… but as a symbol of what… for me… is my more efficient mechanism as an author of "a written- world".

5

***And so... a conversation about Morocco with family members and those black and white photographs... and the glue that the creative act often uses... the past... and its pieces were all I needed.*

Additional marginal notes:

"He had been by the contradictions in his muse's persona: intimate of some details and only vagueness, suspicion and shadows of hints about other ingredients of her make up.
He had to choose early on. Create a fiction based on reality or chance getting more "grit" that had been suggested by family members.

Additional author's notes on Barka: *The Barka persona forced me to confront the painful, geo-political truth. The truth... and the reality [different concepts Writing about a world... is /has always been in between the colonial'... and 'colonized'... our [the writer] brains still able of conceiving ethereal things... in a world of cruelty ... the author became aware that the nature of the 'Barka presence' ...her multi-level, persona: a mother's image and her Berber ancestry i.e. a descendant of the Roman invasion of the land.*

**** *The African continent is a complicated subject that has been fictionalized {e.g. "Out of Africa" by Isak Dinesen [a gentrified British] or in Jean-Marie Le Clezio [le Désert]. In the later, Lalla, the shepherdess, giving birth under a moonlit night in the Sahel {Solinga UConn Dissertation], describes 'love for a setting', that once again, surmounts geo-politics.*

"This unschooled, young woman-shepherdess, taught me more than all my degrees and publishing." [In notes on personal mythologies J-Y.S.]

Days... when time did not exist.
A fable

For a clueless humanity,
in its earliest presence... in so-called:
Time.

Its imprint on things,
must have seemed like those on the sand.

Our worlds... our societies:
Seemingly, still stopping, at the last curve by the river.

Whatever was down that road, would always be there.
Time and space...
would always be there.
With no particular need, to be captured or named,
... in recognition of their apparent eternity.

*****

A time...
before names had been given... to now and later.
A time before...
the invented concepts and relative importance
of this... and or... any other Life.

Of the value of pivotal moments:
Such as giving a lasting hug... and then going out the door.

*Inspired by a photograph of two little girls walking away from the camera into
the solid blue emptiness of a path on the ocean side of Long Island, on a windy
Fall day.*

Lovers in academia

Passionate lovers... and now, arguably... each other's best friend: reunited by circumstances. He... thus, felt trepidation, when her name was announced at the opening of the conference assembly.

It should have been a practical way to see each other:
The anonymous safety of a first-rate symposium.

Papers to present.
Reputations to polish.

Enough intellectual activity...
to keep their animal instincts, otherwise occupied.

Insulated from the other
in their assigned lecture halls.

No mundane concerns:
only the possibility of extra gray hair.
Or some cream-resistant wrinkle, near her lips.

No lack of topics: for small talk:
The continuing hopes and expectations
of advancement and publication, for both.

Not even the fear of decrepitude:
which had been the favorite theme of some of his early writings.

None of these understandingly very human concerns…
did he feel.

———

He did fear... however...
a rekindling of his passion
fed by the ambivalence of her regal glance and leanings.

The fear... of instead… possibly seeing
the image of someone:
to share with that precious person.

Visions of her flesh upon flesh.
And... to his heart-stopping amazement:
Still... not unlike the result of drug-induced hallucinations:

-Out of body flight-
-Weightlessness of his soul-

-A divine dispensation of the rewriting of Genesis-
-A return to the sensual innocence of Paradise, for both.

-One look into her eyes-

And... they were meeting for the first time.
-All again-
Even... "That horrible cafeteria-coffee"!

-And... his... still being part of her intimate life-

Seamlessly sharing the sort of molecular secret:
Which makes for true lovers.

The fastest computer...
"drinking a Café au lait, in Paris"
A poet's reprieve

From "Pages of personal mythologies"... "It is the philosophical battle: between the absolutes: assumed... in a 'godless-universe of the Absurd'... and the unlimited dimensions of [in this instance]... 'Human-love'... that will make for the irreconcilability, of 'the poetic and scientific'. The unyielding, inert solidity of 'dumb space and time'... and the irrationality of human, 'sentient' presence.

***

This poem... a poet's reaction, scribbled, in the re-reading of human-attempts of 'building' a mind.***** It is written with poetic-license, in view of the rapid changes in the budding field of 'Artificial Intelligence'.

The fastest computer...
Could not have reconstructed:

All envies...
All quenched thirsts.

All whispers:
In the silky-cotton sheets, of Maghreban heat.

Every visceral current ever emitted:
by any random tendril, of his mind.

———

The past
-and its future-

...were contained
by the bottomless depth...
behind minute sparkles, on her iris.

The sumptuous cultural setting
became one-dimensional, inert props.

Having glanced at her picture...
... returning him to the cafeteria:****

Surrounded... still... by an intimate:
flinty sensuality.

*** *Increasing evidence, of the existence of microscopic, naturally-occurring, biological-neurons... with the equivalent of thousands of computers... allowing the 'MIND'... to conceive of itself, in many concurrent settings and activities at once. And how we seem... [once again]... arrogantly self-assured, of understanding things... 'having reversed-engineered, from inside these things'. [excerpts from "Notes on Personal Mythologies".*

**** *A very mundane, College-cafeteria: and yet the time of 'their pre-paradisiac expulsion.*

***** *"Mind"... quaint and all-encompassing short-cut term, used in one of the various, multi-paged, internet explanations... attempting to describe the amazing speed and complexity of our million-year-old [squishy, little brain]: that seems to put the narration of the poem... all at once and seamlessly... in that Paris café... that hotel... that bedroom-embrace... those eyes... that primitive, sexual/sensual... olfactory response et al. And to this writing: not yet, any lines of computer-codes available or 'artificially' invented at that sentient level.*

Returning from the atrocities of war

Listening and reflecting about the delusional bravado of former soldiers
"fond memories of their military days".
Ex-colleagues, seemingly unaffected by military savageries.

Impeccable respect for civil order:
Not a speeding ticket in sight.

Irreproachable moral standards, reinforced every Sunday:

Postcard-perfect lives and living.
And the contradiction for one...

of hushed hints and rumors of special-forces hand to hand combat.

Virility of aggression as demanded.
Primordial survival as required
in bloodied, muddy swamps.
And yet…

miraculously, still attached to a sensitive soul.

For the other...

endless references to meteoric rise in ranks
linked to the chemical effectiveness of Agent Orange.

Volubilis **

*A cautionary tale, impressed on a young adolescent, of the impact of climate change. ****

The setting... alignment of hints of a dignified street:
Ghosts of white toga-clad shoppers.

Toddlers and luscious fruits, in mothers' arms.

The screaming contradiction of life and its opposite:
Humanity. Its fragility.
And the resilience of its precious remaining humanism.

———

Presently:
arid surrounding of sand and vipers.
And yet... still existing echoes of thriving millennia-old cultures:

Distant descendants.
Different languages and habits.

Drinking and eating: from local fields with doubtful futures.
Coming. Aggressive emptiness.

Passively waiting for earthly transformation:
Into reddish, Martian landscape.

** *Morocco [circa 1950's]...walking through the ancient, Roman city of Volubilis, North Africa: Enormous, sandstone-skeletons remains of a once, thriving streets.{revisited from "Clair-obscur of the soul}*

*** *"Papa... pourquoi ont-ils construit une ville au milieu du désert"? [Dad... why did they built a city in the middle of the desert?"]*

Religious Sharpshooter

Inspired by an accidental and fictionalized, conversation with a soul-searching military, ex-sharpshooter.

Bar stools...
are akin to the old fashion, church confessionals:
the anonymity is guaranteed by the loud guitar solos
and the alcohol fumes.

Each protagonist had his job description:
The confessant...
a Hollywood-sized, "good old boy" with his destroyed,
Americanized ideals.

And the confessor...
a long-time academic, European-type,
effete absurdist.

The props and scenarios for the classical stage:
the Biblical certainties of a sun crazed Moses
and the babblings of a Ionesco-play.

Cheap tasteless 2.5 beer...
meets Remy Martin Cognac!

The evening was pregnant with issues.
As well, as the rancid smells of overcooked fries.

———

And yet... and yet...
Humanity and humanism are resilient:
having survived worse conditions in the annals of religious atrocities,
and well-meaning cultural genocides.

Thus, the apparent cocoon of silence
that seemed to fall over the odd couple.

It flowed along with a tear-streaked whisper from the special-op officer:

"I could no longer pick up my sniper riffle...
... having seen too many human beings
... looking at me though the crosshairs
...for their last ten seconds of life!"

And humans... discovered the universe **

And humans… discovered the universe:
and in it...

the pieces of a pre-existing
-all-encompassing... swirling of left-overs-
primordial junk!

Humans... having made a home
-not unlike prehistoric families: in prefab Dordogne grottos-
on this planet:
A random, third rock, from a minor star.

————————

And then,
Humanity's marvelous tour de force:
collapsing
-Human's adapted and adaptive explanation-
nomenclature
on these THINGS!

————————

Newtonian... Einstein-like formulae:
neatly tying these quasi, divine forces
on dusty, black boards.

Humanity's very own elegant creation:
Higher Mathematics.

Electrons... for a long while
had been unproductively circling around nuclei,

until humanity used them to power light bulbs.

*** In addition to humans who 'discovered' cures for diseases by giving a name for the process, the author invokes his right to mention on of his favorite animal of La Fontaine's fables the roster who famously 'woke up the Sun' in the morning!*

Comment by a slightly jaded, Ph.D. researcher, on a Krisper-like project: "Origin... what origin? It is not miraculous... it is simply there... it was always there... we simply discovered this thing!"

Powdery happiness
*Ode to Mephisto***

Powdery concentration of hallucinatory happiness:
Beyond the bounds of existential ethics.

But not beyond the culpability,
from very personal, childhood ethics.

———

Not much had changed, since that ride in the ambulance:
In the prime of youth...
... feeling life...
... escaping with every bead of sweat!
... and yet... and still...

The palpable! The available!

The tastes and smells... of earthly goods.

The acrid, sweet-bitterness, of easy things…
and easier beings!

———

A fleeting thought:
Ahh!... To be reincarnated!
In one's own images...
... in the personal genesis, of the created worlds of fiction!

** Grantor of desperate... unattainable... lovers' wishes.

*Parisii** fisherman*

A humanist fable, in honor of the reconstruction of Notre Dame de Paris.

Like a message in a bottle:
He sat in the grayish mud of the gentle river.

In his hands…
… a piece of soft Lutetian-sandstone…

… allowing him to fashion the life-giving,
smooth curves of his pregnant mate.***

————

His innate humanity, mesmerized,
by the sanguine beauty of the watery sunset.

And thus…a secular…
-yet eternal human thought-
made him burrow the fragile avatar of organic life:

The signature … of innumerable artists
-who in the middle of sleepless nights-

Like the arched-stones of Notre Dame,
fight against their nemesis…
… the void of time.

** *Parisii-tribe, fisherman on the left bank of the future city of Paris.*

*** *Reference to Paleolithic [fertility?] statuettes: known as "Venus figurines".*

The fields of innocence 2**
Future couple… Thirty years later

She was between the field of innocence and adulthood… where laid her life.
Somewhere between the light green of the blades of grass…
…and the blue green of her glance.

Eyes of youth…
… and images of a faithful and protective yellow dog.

Somewhere in her heart… exists still…
…this unpretentious little path to a clearing.

This clearing … still in its space, among visions of her younger universe:
The one, still empty of the future hurt and loneliness from Others.

"Moon River…*** wider than a mile…"

It is a time and a place full of potential and dreams.
Timid awareness of timidity.

Flowering femininity…
A time of spiritual ease amidst the common… yet eternal beauty of things of
the earth.

Just a field… to the privileged few****…allowed along her hidden path.

More precious now, than her goldish hair then:
For IT lives…
in the precious whiteness of innocence of the past.

"Moon River… wider than a mile…"

———

Gone is the Madonna-like hair… on a doll-like frame.
A young girl… doing young things:
in the protocol of life… and the unwelcomed pressure of the rites of passage.

"Moon River… wider than a mile…"
On the other side… she faced the harsh solidity of the demands of reality and society.

And so… between the field of innocence… and the age of remembrance:
we find that we have left the best behind…
…somewhere in the blades of grass…
…and the disappearing footsteps in the early frost.

All that remain… of the field… of the shy frogs… of the grayish rock next to the brook…
…are the crying strings of violins… and an almost feminine tenor voice…
…on a scratchy vinyl record.
"Moon River… wider than a mile…"

A young woman, on a stroll through the fields of her parents' house before leaving towards her life.

Original version in "Clair-obscur of the Soul" Jean-Yves Vincent Solinga [chapter 6: Between the Friend and the Lover].

** Original text modified as: "The Fields of innocence 2" in post "Black Butterfly Dust"/ in "A Bee in Monet's Garden".

*** "Moon River" favorite song of the young woman.

**** Expression [Happy Few] used in English, by Marie-Henri Beyle (Stendhal) who wrote some of the most insightful passages, in literature, about love.

*Pêcheur Parisii***

Une fable humaniste, en l'honneur de la reconstruction de Notre Dame de Paris.

Comme un message dans une bouteille :
Il s'assit sur la boue grise de la tranquille rivière.

Dans ses mains…
… un morceau de grès Lutétien…
… lui permettant de représenter
la douceur des courbes, fertiles et sinueuses, de sa compagne enceinte. ***

———

Son humanité innée, hypnotisée
par la beauté écarlate du coucher de soleil humide.
Et donc…
une pensée séculaire
-et pourtant éternelle-
Lui fit creuser dans le fragile avatar de la vie organique :

La signature …   d'innumérables artistes
-qui dans des nuits sans sommeil-
Comme les arches de pierre de Notre Dame
Se battent contre leur némésis.…
… le vide temporel.

** *Les Parisii : tribues gauloises qui habitaient sur les rives de la Seine.*
*** *Référence aux statuettes Paléolithiques [de la fertilité] connues sous le nom de "Figurines de Vénus".*

Paris: "Birth of Venus" **

Paris: Fontaine Saint Michel. 1981celebration of François Mitterand's election.

He felt paralyzed:
Having jumped, fully-clothed, in the fountain-font:
She ...emerged a Goddess.

"This city is indeed magical":
He whispered to himself.

The banks of simple light bulbs -
from the North-African restaurants
gave a surrealist dimension to her hips...

This place
spoke of biblical fertility and privileged grounds:
Where humanity, is one with earthy happiness.

Seemingly giving him
a temporary divine dispensation:

The right to re-enter the heavenly gates
that keep away the mundane detritus of living.

Making this young man... one of the chosen.
Called the "Happy few" by Stendhal.

———

He remained breathless in front of this cottony vision:
Made of her floral and fleshy transparency.

Now a concrete reminder
of the fleeting nature of lyrical moments.

Memories of an American, former college-age expatriate of the Viet Nam War.

** *Lyrical overlap of "Nascita di Venere ["The Birth of Venus"]by Sandro Botticelli and the wild celebrations at the Saint Michel fountain...with this quasi-religious, translucent femininity, of a student, in the middle of its "font".*

Life... in the Cosmos, is not normal...the opposite is.

Whatever life-form...
... humanity...
will acquire, in its evolution.

With whatever life-forms...
it will interact.

In whatever dimension
it will survive...
...
... the cosmos will exhibit
an absolute disinterest, for its presence.

———

And, if our 'Big Bang'
is one of many...

... the process will repeat itself: meaninglessly...
... into its infinity.

And maybe... just maybe...
an awareness of these mild neuronic impulses** of one brain...
Could spread as an alternate poetic, (re) Genesis.

Leading to other human*** forms:
Sitting peacefully: on a paradisiac island,

-In the middle of an enormous ocean-
-Looking at an enormous sunset-

Where... in its previous life...
These powdery-sands had been turned into glass:
Under enormous thermonuclear blasts.

**In the English language: in this reincarnation of the author.

*** Or any other sentient form,

A child's smile

*Mettez-le sur mes genoux ** [rue Paradis, Marseille]*

Whiffs of humanity:
Like hints of Spring flowers through the prison bars;
do indeed… survive inhumanity.

The unsoiled smile of a child:
Somehow, rekindling hours of family, in Alpine outings.

The drab, olive-green of the military uniform.
No protection for the young German.

And thus, this, recalled, post-war,
family-tale of ambivalence:
A mother's respectful appreciation and contradictory, nagging sense.

-Mixture of morsels of common humanity-
Within sight of the Gestapo headquarters building.

-Ironically… on rue Paradis,*** in Marseille-

** *"He can sit on my knees" German soldier, to a French mother, offering to hold her little boy, in a crowded Marseille tramway (the occupying-troops had priority-sitting).*

*** *Rue Paradis was the headquarters of the Gestapo.*

Inlaid Memories of the Maghreb.

Inlaid memories of the Maghreb:
Incrusted in a Wooden cabinet;
A long way from the Chella of its birth.

Silent companion of exodus from the semi-tropical warmth of its birth.
Born among the acrid smells of crispy sardine skins.
The hypotonic rapid Morish beat.
And plaintive flutes.

Just a simple furniture piece:
With the magical sorcery of its Thuya wood,
Ability to capture time in its filigree of arabesques.

Lost to mother land.
Exiled along with a family's Exodus...

——

It had been there… always…
In quiet exotic solidity:

Reddish nuances of Thuya wood inlays.
As though still transcribing
Its intoxicating birth.

Intertwined into yellow accented swirls:
Seemingly capturing, in its silent wooden way...
... Its calvary-stations:
To its retuned, privileged status.

Theme of the poem inspired by the 'Provenance' of furniture pieces, built in the 'Chella' of Salé, Maroc. (circa 1950).

Like the silver candelabras of "les Misérables-fame"… this quasi-religious icon of the 'stations-of-the-family' Odyssey… had come close to becoming abandoned, in a frozen backyard of the 'New World'. [it now lords over my house, underneath the thermostat!]

Cosmological odds

Near Bormes-les-mimosas (Provence)

Overlooking the Mediterranean:
Sentient lives… in the Classical sun.

Warmth of their flesh…
… now her flesh…
and remains of agnostic, rays of sunshine.

This intertwined couple
-unwilling entities-
In this earth-bound ballet.

————

They will be filled with the vibrant memories:
-the noble, vibrant arrogance of youth-

That is…
the feeling of a big bang
-accompanied with its background of warmth-

Frissons of joy.
And very simply… KNOWING IT!

Marginal note regarding this poem, in the author's "Pages of a personal mythology" [Upon a return trip to France on the occasion of my retirement, I found myself surrounded by hillsides covered by mimosas trees... in February: which I attributed as an honor to myself!]

Ceremonial Wine

Recalling, a religious service, in Nasi-Occupied France, when the altar-boys added water to the ceremonial wine.

Cast of greater-than-life characters:
Worthy of Fernandel and Pagnol movies.**

Deprived, sickly youngsters.
Years of shortages.

Fear of bombs from the air.
And booby-trapped objects, on the ground.

And these altar-boys!
Boys first.
Angels second.

Temptation of religious-service wine:
Aggravated by empty stomachs!

With an added portion of
Devilish, inebriated, mischievousness and youthful temptation.

———

Poor parish: in lavender and pine-scented Maquis-hills.
Hard life of sheep herders… with now,
Deadly, highway-controls.

Weird presence of recalcitrant husbands:
now joining Sunday religious services and church fairs
subterfuge for underground contacts.

Misery all around:
And this balm from… the healthy, rebellious laughter
-Around the venerable table-
made of chestnut-tree wood, from the hills.

Post-World Two, family tales… that, in retrospect, encapsuled so well the human soul: the overlap of laughter and tears. The altar-boys, recalling the hilarious grimace, on the celebrating-priest, as he tasted the substituted, watered-down wine… amidst the war-time conditions of starvation-rationing.

** Stage-name of French comic actor of early twenty century who excelled in the tragic-comic personae: in particular wartimes. As well as, Marcel Pagnol who captured the Provençal soul.

Eternity and Propofol

A routine, medical intervention, needing a 'light sedation' of Propofol

A minor diversion... of one's slippage
into the useful literary 'bogeyman':
... Death.

Death... one of few philosophical, shortcuts:
Humanity's concepts of an absolute...
... any absolute!

Death and its unavoidability:
The antidote to endless, seminar discussions.

The last stop toward... and just before...
... ad absurdum.

"No one... on this side of an absurd universe**...
has ever enlighten us".

———

Thus... these few seconds, looking at the attending staff...
-before full consciousness-
... mumbling...
"This is the way, that I want to die."
"Seamlessly."

** *Statement of agreement, from the corner of the seminar table. The subject,
at hand: a deity-free cosmos. "A bee in Monet's garden."*

HIS allegory of love, in the Louvre

A former academic, revisiting one of his favorite sculptures, in The Louvre.

She must have emerged
completely formed from the vitreous matter.

She is, in her plasticity,
the acquired human freedom, of post-paradisiac sensuality.

"This one...is you":
He shyly whispered.

"The one that captured, so naturally
-in its Limoges white-translucence-
the lubricity and reserve
of true goddesses."

Granting him, on his pillow,
eternal wisps of her.

A.I. Destroyed the University, Saturday-Night "Blind Date"

Reflections, by a 1960's University graduate, about how Artificial Intelligence would have invaded and changed his memories of his dating experiences.

"You have your brother's eyes."

He was the "Blind Date" whisperer:
Always willing to accept the rebellious sister.

To ignore what would have been
the misogynous internet-death of a gentle-red head.

The girl on the rebound.
The eccentric artist…
the unknown, trauma, nursing-major from New York.

Last minute panicked classmate
with enigmatic visiting sister:
"Please help me:
I trust you with my sister and my car!"

Pre-internet. Pre-everything days…
When height of the date was fuzzy and optimistic:

[She turned out to be a forward on her basketball team].
His ambitious five-three… to her majestic six-three.
….
… But missing her mother's Italian dishes…
… and intrigued by his knowledge of French cooking.

———

Pre-internet,
dark spaces of unknowns of unknowns… on both sides!

His quirky… seamless…
… natural-European handshake.

His scandalous…for the times…
… bise.**

———————

All this trepidation of possibilities and discoveries:
Destroyed…
by instantaneous… biographical… intimate details of…
everything… about Everything:
Before HER appearance.

Coming down… the stairs:
From the off limit… sanctum sanctorum
of the upper levels of the women's dorm.

** *Bise: an affectionate kiss.*

From his personal journal: " A.I. has made impossible, the moment when he first saw her coming down the stairs of her dormitory… in today's world, I would have known EVERYTHING about her before-hand. Instead, the night turned out to be an unexpected stroll, into her world [our worlds] of emotional dimensions… untranslatable into artificial computer codes.

SCIF **

A classroom-experiment ***

*In the very far future of A.I..: we could conceivably have "educated individuals"
who will not know how to write anything (unimpeachably original).*

*In this 'thought-poem': an unannounced classroom activity: a "reconstructed"
model, of a traditional, 1970's, twelfth-grade, high school or first year, university-
level: writing exercise. The classroom setting; old fashion distribution of blue-
books; with number two pencils; announcement of roughly 'one hour' in order
to "write about a known-topic studied during the course: "Love(s)" [in this
case] … use any number, of love-themed passages, in the course or beyond.*

*[nota bene: a SCIF-like space, is with no functioning signals possible and no
personal electronic instruments].*

Panic-filled minutes:
Very adept… very bright…

-selected and self-selected-

Communicative individuals,
"Authors" of produced strings…
Reams, upon reams… of smartly coded thoughts!

And now… having to …
Organically…
… generate a human-based statement.

Love…
in its multi-social and endless hues of colors:
-to would make a "Monet envious"!

———

Looking over the attentive, surprised faces.
Mind-bending, innovative dimensions,
take hold in their squishy, neuron-filled, human brains!

———

Now facing the blank pages of
the "feared examination, bluebook".

———

Time to…
Transfer. Present. Prioritize…
Humanly filtered and acquired knowledge.

———

The first moments of terror over;
The wager is…
that the individual will rediscover…
… will re-experience the cosmological.

-The quasi-miraculous value-
-The evolutionary miracle-
-The incomparable beauty of the human dimension-

Of the unscripted.
The uncoded.
The ethereally-eternal.
The weight of the universe represented …
by that wrinkled love note…
from that hazel-eyed, grammar-school student, behind you.

** *SCIF: a designated "spy-proof" room. [a.k.a. Sensitive compartmented information facility]*

*** *This poem is the author's reaction to having been shown an iPhone screen, of his house-guest [with only two or three foot-note names from the dissertation… presenting him [in minutes] … a very good, two-page-outline of what his PhD Abstract [which took him years of research] could have looked like.*

"She cleans our house"

His budding understanding of English
-in the chaotic, high school, lunchroom conversation-
Made him alert for recognizable
phonic clues…

Pieces of clues… any clues!
Associated to his uneasy presence at this table.***

_____

His mother's geographical and very cultural, first-name
had stood out, in the conversation…
apparently about him.

That friendly… precious… familial Provençal sound…
The one from his father to his mother:
Around the garlicky background of a kitchen in the past.

The whole… floating in a sea
of unpronounceable new diphthongs of the present.

_____

A string of smiling clueless, acknowledgements, on his part…
must have been seen as approval of the topic:

The "new immigrant"
at the table.

No calumnious rumors…
No lies or insults.
It was rather…
… the matter-of-fact nature of his mother's job.

… "Oh, his mother…
She's our new maid."

*** *Lunch table, at an American high school.*

Nota bene: in an unspoken, exquisite symbiosis; the "ladies [several of whom… fervent Orthodox Jews] had been affected by World War Two nasi-camp, and general antisemitism] wanted to be supportive: by hiring the financially strapped, older, newly arrived, immigrant [the later, ironically, a fervent Roman Catholic].

Voyage through Oppenheimer's mind

Comment by university colleague regarding sentient life:" Life is, unfortunately, more like a play with no script or director."

Endowed (as of this writing) with one of the latest versions, on the evolutionary scale, of "a human brain" ... the following are personal reflections on J. Robert Oppenheimer: the singularly, iconic figure of humanity's introduction to the nuclear age and its threat to humanity.

The designated head of the Manhattan Project, Oppenheimer was quoted, voicing his unease with their invention...
"Now I am become Death, the destroyer of worlds".
["The quotation 'Now I am become death, the destroyer of worlds', is literally the world-destroying time," explains Thompson, adding that Oppenheimer's Sanskrit teacher chose to translate "world-destroying time" as "death", a common interpretation. Its meaning is simple: irrespective of what Arjuna does, everything is in the hands of the divine.]

This voyage allows a speculative look
at what Oppenheimer would have said about turning over,
...decisive moments...
of the future of sentient life on the globe...
... over to Artificial Intelligence and its lines of codes.

An endless topic:
but Oppenheimer, for many observers,
is a nexus of pure sciences and a prophet for a sustainable humanism.

-A convenient starting point-

In him, we have a superb -non-silicon- organic, human-mind:
Looking into the first nuclear cloud:
Symbolizing
sentient nothingness.

That is… the opposite of a sterile, third rock, from the Sun.
A planet that had evolved Amino acid.
The building blocks
of self-awareness.

Making humanity,
-descendants of these rocks…
…know…
that they used to be just…
… rocks.

———

Hence, this pseudo-academic, lyrical travel through the privileged
scientific mind of a gentle, pipe-smoker.

Sitting, maybe at the head of a seminar table
Maybe the eternal discussion
on Plato's vaporous idealism
versus
Machiavelli's solid, no-nonsense realism.

Mankind encased in muddy, daily political survival…
Still looking for heavenly clues.

———

_Having invented these codes?
_Did we remove? … could we remove?
… Potentially dangerous human factors
from the decision-making in the equation?

Would… in extremis… AI-built by humans
final … unappealable decision-making?

Which avenue would the code writers have
a quasi-divine status of infallibility and deniability
or…
escape responsibility:
the mortal sin of Existentialists.

———

Humanity is facing a cosmic wager, with AI:
our very own, modern-day,
Faustian bargain:

At stake the possible destruction of the cosmic miracle
that WE are.

———

The question remains:
Although, humanity is the very smart descendant
of very smart hirsute, cave animals:
We are animals nevertheless!

With remaining molecular memories
of beastly-rut, unproductive, jealousy-driven emotions.
Dangerous decisions of wounded egos, from executive meetings.

———

All these quaint human attributes
Could be sprinkled in the frigidity of AI-codes;
Which are NOT musical score of notes
for the "Afternoon of a Fawn".

Can we forewarn AI misinterpretation
-by a machine-
Not appreciating the poetic license of the deadly words and violent acts of
Greek tragedies?

———

Would AI differentiate among the aberrations
-still beyond human comprehension-
of the existence of extermination camps?

Torture chambers; or death by melted lead for regicide…
Often… from otherwise, civilized people?

———

Enters, stage left, the "Wizard of Oz".

Humanity gravitates to these straw-men figures:
With uncanny ability to soak-up our problems.

Quasi-mythologically, untraceable revered figures,
that guide us by the hand.
Wise men … enlightened… or lost desert shepherds.

Uncompromising… unerring leaders ready to sacrifice your sons.

Hall-of-mirrors of soporific worlds.

"En attendant Godot" [
turning out to be… after all… not more than a pleasant night at the
theatre:
Godot will not show up.

And stepping outside on the side walk
-the calming, sensual figure-
Of Albert Camus…
whispering… lyrically about human solidarity:
… next to a bikini-clad Marie.

… no one is in charge… more correctly and all encompassing…
NOTHING is in charge.

University, late-night, bull-session [revised version]
A fable

Post-doc. scientist researcher, on evolutionary genetics: daydreaming in
front of data on his computer screen.

Was his guilty conscience…
the result of his university's "humanities requirements"?

All he had wanted to do,
is pure, unadulterated, scientific research!

He was forced, instead to study…
Such Odysseys … as chasing some recalcitrant whale!

Greek or roman regicides.
Unhappy, incestuous wives, princesses or demented Caesars.

———

Interesting tales of humans…
doing human things!

Studying and reflecting, on all these tales:
Probably, in order to make sense of our imperfections.

———

All of these studies by day:
Followed by late-night bull-sessions!!
-Some, accentuated with one's favorite accelerant-

———

In the meantime

-untethered to the unending, need for research funds-
… in dreams, research lived freely.

———

And so… we have our evolutionary winners:
-HUMANS-

The smart monkeys.
Collective trashing. Land-abuse and disrespect.
Earth on fire!
This unique, cosmological wonder!

———

A voice…
[from the assembled, inebriated, science-dormitory group]

"The ELEPHANTS!…
… with their herd-protection instincts…
should have won!
Simply won… and not evolved.

"Putting, all of us… out of work!"

Aegean sighs
Near Mitiline.

Homage to James Baldwin.

Like trying to encapsulate
the sound of intimate conversations;
of intimate couples.

Quasi-nuptials.
Of collective echoes:
on historic neo-classical facades.

———————

Side-street, labyrinth of cafés:
still busy, near a summer midnight.

Palpable sensuality ...
... freely expressed.

Bodily ease...
... of very-knowing, personal gestures.

Scandalously short, European skirts.
Men... in smart, flank-hugging,
effeminizing, suit-jackets.

Minds and bodies:
Seemingly, synchronously living,
in the same earthly paradise....

... that is...
a human tendency, for the sparkling,
most sanguine apple...
still hanging in the local museums.

———————

He had left behind...
the wooden, moralizing undertones, of his New England home.
With wooden,
late 1950's, television families:
in quandaries about mother's new haircut.

———

While, Gitanes smoking
-Audrey Hepburn-inspired-
women
... peopled the terrasses!

But... but...
It was, specifically,
Her severe, coupe-à-la garçonne**
which stigmatized his soul forever!

A sort of illumination
into her complex, inner worlds and spaces!

Not a member of the happy few:
She never confided the source, of her hints of ambivalence.

** *Her extremely short "coupe à la garçonne" made her, ironically more feminine in his eyes.*

Late 1960's, "Expat", G.I., in Paris.

Wishing to be a cork-screw

The gesture had all the bravado...
the shameful, male... self-reflection...
of her presence in his arms.

A solid ... indestructible object:
Dual. Shiny. Thick plated arms.
Unbeatable against
the most noble Bordeaux Châteaux!

——

All he could dream about...
... was the pedestrian function, of this inanimate thing.

The ultimate insult was...
-That instigated by a meal-
-With his beautiful family and academists friends-

Culturally perfect ambiance:
Accompanied by culinary taste.

With all these tangible reasons:
For immediate and concrete happiness.

.....

... All he could think about:
were her warm slender fingers: around... hers!

Former visiting professor, reflecting on 'cultural', parting gift [twin to his own]... to his former colleague.

My father the 'porter' ***

"There is a quiet dignity in this man": Comment by executive-office, staff member, of large pharmaceutical firm... about a new immigrant porter.

Having read all of Alexandre Dumas'** novels...
... one wonders if that broomstick had become his sword:
his protection against words....

The hurtful-simplicity ... of hurtful words.

———

Having lived, wartime, Nazi occupation.
And now... assiduously following,
the chemical-protocol of the research-laboratories.

Now wearing, the coarse-weave, garment of a porter:
Having been disrobed of his musket, sword and multi-colored silk-pants.

-Military background and overall strong nerves-

Having steeled him, when overhearing inquiries,
such as :
"Does he know how to read?"

** *Alexandre Dumas père [father]: author of "The Three Musketeers".*

*** *Fictionalized for poetic license.*

Ladybug, 42 floors up

Even the unbridled themes of the program "Suits," of Netflix fame, did not include a ladybug [yes... the insect!] visiting the 42nd floor office-window of an investment firm: with breathtaking views of Manhattan and the Hudson River.

Manhattan.
Breaking news!

Not the U.S President, coming into town.
Not a bus, full of unwashed humanity:
But the quasi-miraculous visits, by this fragile insect.

If only, she had been bearer of wisps of eternal, summer breezes!
Lightness of soul and child-like, insouciance!

No... instead:
-on the air-conditioned side, of the floor-to-ceiling glass-

... the beautiful glance, of the beautiful viewer** ...
... is an adult mix...
of endless, spreadsheets-lists, accounts receivable and touchy, personnel issues.

———————

But somehow: this little beast
-like a selfless Messiah-

Appears to absorb all the anxieties of the adult world.

So... that for a few precious seconds,
the high-stakes... high-wire world of finance...

becomes a vision of HER crippled butterfly
-religiously-fed with sugared water-
upon her return from grade school.

** *Since "beauty" seems to be a prerequisite for "Suits".*

Epiphany from the depths of a Nihilistic-Hedonism
A fable

These thoughts, triggered by the continuing headlines of worldwide heat records and other existential threat to humanity... and a sigh towards the "cosmological miracle of those glorious wines".

Our anthropologically leaning gods of literatures;
The ones with a striking similarity
to our quaint human weaknesses...

―――――

... must have, all along, been approving of our bacchanalian enjoyment
"of the joys of life" ... on Earth.

These forward-looking deities,
all-knowing and full of wisdom,
had anticipated our appetites:

Making possible, such things as
Moulin à vent... Gigondas ... Fleury wines
... to exist!

Smart monkeys, that we are, allowing us,
to discover the effects of fermented juices from grapes,
in the Mediterranean heat.

―――――

It turns out that these gods,
find themselves, in turn, living,
in a godless universe.

Prisoners...
themselves of their own freedom.
...and like us...
... not able, to NOT be free.

Leaving both our lines and welfare...
depending on the whims of the only entity available:
Our Humanity.

** *Vines*

*** *Docteur Rieux, of Albert Camus', "La peste"... who bravely and solitarily stands up to the plague.*

49

The reality... behind the lyricism **
Deconstruction of a personal Muse

Before disappearing, from the solidity of his daily life:
she had transformed into a veil
of vaporous presence in his soul.

She had become, both quivering flesh
and also, acquired the sensual immobility of Grecian marble.

Craving for both,
he started to fill the void with words.

———

Her touches, now, living in the synesthesia of her
favorite French parfum.

The nobility, of blue-veined curves, in the Mediterranean stone
of his lecture-slides... would, at times,
cause him a personal pause...
... bringing forth...
acrid, sensual emanations, from crimson flesh.

———

Still haunted, years later,
by her transfixing, dark glance from her pillow.

Searching... right and left... for the precious, anticipated next seconds:
Impregnating him, deep into his soul,
with a virile scowl, full of her worries and sadness:

These human emotions of mere mortals...
... gave this deity in his arms...
the complexity of grandes dames of tragedies:

-A susceptibility and a mortal's acknowledgement of time-

———

No absolutes... seemed to have ever been created...
... outside of their embrace.

No extension of the now: into eternity.
Except for the deluded, religious prophecies
from the desert shepherds
of their academic fields.

———

This is when,
in the silence of the darken-room.
This is when...
her flesh made of molecules of ideals.
This is when...
she fell into... where all dreams come to die:

-The prosaic... the chronological-

She wore openly,
her post paradisiac ... mere-mortal ... earthy stigmata.

All and everything.
In that one person. That one body.

The duality of flesh
and the quasi-miraculous...
cosmological, consciousness, attached to it.

The human mind's own: secular... intermediary...
... god-like creativity...
to think... to perceive in metaphors...***

To see... to see beyond the real stains on the sheets.
Those made with the unalterable ink, of real lovers:
on lumpy, miniscule, Parisian, mattresses.

————

Far away now, in time and space.
Far from the time-cured paints of classical Masters:
this deity,
cried real tears in front of his teary eyes.

She spoke of urban realities:
"Pretty girl in ugly streets."

Cold winters:
fighting city, morning-traffic.

"Intrusive" ... lecherous landlord:
In the role of a Claude Rollo.

––––––––––

And her...
still a vision of perfection!
Tired aching feet: from perfect shoes.
Noble demeanor.
Unforced, divine, daily comportment:
Modest genesis...
And such worldly conquest!

Muddy knees.
Brushing blackish-snow off of her car...
Nothing of all this, taking anything away
from her eventual, reincarnated
perfection, in his lyricism.

** *Deconstruction: memories of a personal Muse [originally, in Notes on personal Mythologies.*

*** *Metaphors and similar literary tools [FELT in the reader's mind], which, this author believes, will be the last hold-out-refuge, for artists and poets, from the Artificial-Intelligence universe.*

The human ability... to create eternal moments. **

It is when these worlds are in complementary equilibrium
- one person... versus society-
-the first-person singular... versus plural-

The lonely artist at his desk
-versus his audience in a full theatre-
...
... that the words...
... the painting...
...the artistic expression...

... break out, of the solidity of the present...

Linking...
that breathless future-moment
to someone's past.

** *The artistic world, creating its own laws of 'malleable' universe: in this case.*

"The kitchen scene... in the play... was eerily, invasively, viscerally... similar to my own." {From the author's: "Introductions to personal mythologies"}.

Lovers in an agnostic universe

Fictionalized professionals, meeting for their first time, at a conference: starting in the morning of the attacks on the Twin Towers in New York... and their illicit, doubly, guilt-ridden but... continuing relationship.

Unknow to each other:
in the vastness of the buildings....

... they had become
their own, unexpected comets.

Bringing, by their combined presence...
-at various intervals in their life-
... resurging, repeated, explosions
of contradictory feelings:

Interspaced by the dull opacity
of what can be existence.

———————

The balance of his time,
leaving him craving for their tête-å-tête, small talk.
And precious remnants of their introductory meeting.

Moments in their lives:
pregnant with a strange, quasi-nuptial privacy,
admits conference-hall confusion.

They had somehow built
-in the corner of a glass and steel cafeteria-
their own bilingual cocoon.

A construction: made of fumes
of paradisiac exceptionalism.

And... on his side:
an un-apological... Faustian drive.

_____

Collective insanity:
-a feeling of 'end of time' apocalypse-

Human beings,
throwing themselves in the crystalline blue
of this early September day.

Somehow. Miraculously.
Nothing. Nothing.
Nothing... could perturb the infinite serenity
of their reciprocal glances:

Glances ...
full of infinite futures ... and fertility.
Futures... and fertility.

Based on "Notes of personal mythologies." ["Famous love stories, of famous couples of world literature... or simply, two of your office colleagues... seem to sometimes live and evolve, in a world of their own realities and ethics... thus seemingly insulating their lives. This "thought poem" puts these individuals in the center of one of the most destructive [and documented] emotional event of history. In "Notes of personal mythologies"]

Windsor knot

The college, rite-of-passage, de rigueur:
"Meeting the roommate's parents".

In a universe of strangers:
the very promiscuity with a roommate,
made him feel less... odd.

Tiny university room:
akin to his physics' class, textbook... on nuclear experiments.

———————

-Using his best vocabulary-
Conversation... with this comfortable, middle-class family:

-Feeling like an inquisition-

He could not contain...
... a bitter envy.

-A hurtful. Personal attack!-

———————

Until the preparation, for the university-house diner:

When the 'American' roommate...
(like, some proud father)
... reached for his very best... very personal tie...

...and in a natural... seamless gesture...
tied the silk, into the famous
afore-mentioned:

-Windsor knot-

... around, his stupefied, roommate's collar!

"Welcome, to your new country!"
He said in an official tone... and a hand shake.

Fictionalized reconstruction, of the symbols of true friendship, shown to 'the outsider'. This... during his University, Freshman-year, which played a double role in his life: as a finishing-school of his introduction to this 'American' culture; as well as, the world of higher academia.

If nothing else matters...

Speculation, on what drives artists and poets to continue. ***

If nothing else matters:
then everything matters.

The slightest pieces of the past and future
ARE all that matters.

Like a modern-day Job
-in front of his goddess-
you feel naked and without pretension.

Your very pores are communicating with things:
You have become an empty vessel...
... ready to accept the magic-mash, made of the dirt of the world.

The very stuff that will ferment into
what makes it worthwhile for you
to be the only thing between an amoeba
and the stellar grandness of a "thinking thing".

———

And in spite of your doubt
about the exact literary position of (such abstractions) as the
... narrative-narrator
... void or human solidarity...
and

in spite of one's exact position on...
... Humans and humanity.
... The spectrum that spans the nausea of the solid world.
... The exaltation of religious revelations...

... you know deep down that
what you have to say... is better than saying nothing.

So, better transferring...
... these moments,
... these words,

...

... to the blackboard of the future
and let the students in on it.

*** *Another venture: to overlap Blaise Pascal's "Hidden God" and Albert Camus et al. ... godless universes: in "Notes/Cahiers on 'Personal Mythologies'/ 'Mythologies personnelles': Prompted by an encouraging [dolce voce] comment by a lingering student on the way out of class: ... "Don't give up... I love what you have to say!"*

[nota bene: there are purposefully, no temporal indicators in the body of the poem]

Hitting Bottom
Writing: when the personal Muse is long gone.

When the object of desire is reduced
-to black points-
on the white and blue, Microsoft-flatness.

That is when, the essence of feeling, is cooked up
in the bowels of a personal hell.

You find yourself...
Scraping, the dry residues of yesterday.

You lick them: like some block of salt
-on par, with a thirsty cow-
back from the pasture.

———

What an image!
She...
... the goddess of your world...
... has become akin to this white dry powder,
that bites into your tongue.

And then.... a sharp sensation!
It transports you.
...
You put down the glass of Chardonnay de Cluny;
and you start to listen to the effervescence inside of you.

This dried up, shred of memory,
is the most potent... most precious drive... that you have ever felt.

She is now, reduced to her very essential ingredients.
The sort of intensity of taste
that goes beyond the moment.

It stays. It enters your memory bank.
The kind of taste that you can reconstruct at will:
Later... on your palate.
Synesthesia: reconstructing HER... through her favorite Maghreban dish.

.

The Lilliputians, infecting the Cosmos

Astronaut Colonel Taylor (Charlton Heston) slamming his fists into the sand, shrieking, "You maniacs! You blew it up! Damn you! [Originally written by: Pierre François Marie Boulle.]

He was our university's dormitory: designated "House Atheist"**. A marvelously bright individual: he was our "Artificial Intelligence"... before its time... and a pleasant personality... that 'humanized' him [to boot]!! Needless to say, that extrapolating and bringing humanity's issues, into the deep future, might have made him wish for a god-like [omnipotent deity] to discipline us!

A sort of cosmic race has opened:
China is interested*** in a 'presence'
On the South Pole of the Moon!

-Water, could be present, underground!-

And so... we are off to the races!
Long live, our Lilliputians needs and brains.

-Delusional pride... and self-assessment-

We will bring our geopolitical problems
to places...
that are now miniscule dots on thermal, telescope-receptors.

The Lilliputians are coming!

** *In "Notes on "Personal Mythologies" J-Y.S.*

*** *CBS Radio broadcast t[circa 2023] concerning China's plans to colonize the Moon for its natural/mineral value.*

We liberated "a" camp...

First-year, High School teacher: first non-teaching, assignment-post: 'surveying'
a sixty-foot wide…"hallway-duty"… at the entrance of huge multi-door cafeteria.

Wide-eyed petrification:
These kids are huge!

Expertise…
… in early Nineteenth Century, French Romantism seemed optional!
And yet… and yet… at times…
-wisdom and eternal truths-
… can be whispered in the boredom of an empty hallway.

———

As part of our hall-way conversation
and his World War Two experience:
My colleague added:
"During his World War Two service?"
"My company was one of the first to get to the concentration-camps."

———

As a rejoinder to our European-pasts:
"Yes, I was with Patton."
"Yes, I saw IT… from the turret of my tank."
"No, no… no more shooting."

———

It was the incongruity of this gentle…
always impeccably dressed…
veteran teacher. *.. and U.S. Army Mechanized… Company Commander.

Bespectacled… three-piece suits:
Now. Simply, my colleague…
…
… who then disappeared…
… in the students' rush, for sloppy-joes and chips.

*Fictionalized character.

A beautiful Baby

Proud grandmother: caring for her grandchild, in pastoral Beaujolais: at the end of the nineteenth century. He would die, in the unimaginable obscenity of World War One, fields; that turned, this cosmic, corner [a quasi-miraculous, evolutionary-gem] into Hell.

Grandchild, for a new century.
Village, in land of plenty.

Plump chickens and velvety milk.
Ordered life, of hardworking people:
In seamless, multi-generational, households.

No luxuries and no vacations.
Instead, sleepy Sunday sermons: from well-meaning priest.

Boisterous drinks, at the local bar:
The future Nouveau-Beaujolais:
Having arrived from the local hills!

Recurring rumors: of some price-hikes for coal.

The boring routine, of endless cycles of routine.
While sturdy farmhouse walls, somehow kept the outside out...
... and the inside continuous.

––––––––

Hints, of Germanic unrest and various, patriotic demands...
... scoffed at...
... as unnatural interference with the grape harvest.
But this grandchild,
would thrive in the new century!

Would be the master
of all matters... down to the stonewall border:
And no need: "For what is beyond".

————

A day came...
that took the grandchild away.
And sent him...
to a hell-hole of shredded flesh.

She could see! She could feel!
This grandmother said...
"she could still touch... his fingers"...
... that had fingered
... the white nectar of the first milking, of the day.
FINGERS...
... now frozen, on a rifle trigger.

————

She could somehow, hear her name, on his lips.
-The way, he would whimper...during an earache.-

But this time: a grand mother's love,
would be set adrift: in the non-human slime:

Part of the outer-galactic term of
... Geo-politics.

Trichterfeldschneise / Sounds of Nature

*To the looped: YouTube [65 Seasons Video Creation], piano version...
'Trichterfeldschneise' of "I'll be seeing you".*

The quasi-amorous hesitation, in the fingering of the keys.
The organic, alternate, ebb and flow, of the musical phraseology:

Naturally echoing each other:
Not unlike a lover's anticipated, coordinated...
... skimming of her flesh...
and then... instead...
nothing... nothing, but the hot breath...
of the virile, vibrations... from the metallic innards
of the grand-piano, sound box:
answered by cascading pearls.

Dexterous fingertips... titillating the ivory-skin of the keys:
Like a high priest...
Mesmerized, in front of an altar of jewels.

-More-precious, than-mere jewels.
-More eternal than his faith.
-More solid than diamonds.
-More immediate, more invasive, than the acrid smells of incense.

Molecules of beauty:
Absorbed by the Grecian-stone, of nature's temples.

————

Outside... on the blinding Mediterranean...
... the limitless birthing of disincarnated sounds.

Returns us, to our cosmological birth:
-From inert-star, granules...
-To everything-
-Everything-

-To our destiny-
-To our sentient longing of being-

Ethereal notes, filling the voids, of our very existence.

A timid world...
...waiting for our human consciousness of living...
... to in turn, give its... acknowledgment...
through this musical perception.

A time... before time:
with no word...yet...
for time itself.

....

Nothing:
but... her slender fingers... stroking his hair.
Her precious... whispered sighs:
... chiseling their names ...
... for future lovers...
... into the cacophony of Parisian traffic.

**The compositor/the pianist: in this solo, with orchestra.*

*Inspired by 'Sounds of nature' YouTube. Piano piece, of "I'll be seeing you...":
with very light, orchestral background. In German: "Trichterfeldschneise"
[sounds of nature]. In "Notes on personal mythologies": "The gods... have
infused, musical poetic-artistry, in this composition!" {J-Y.S}.*

Death... humanity's ultimate solidarity

Life," he [Albert Camus] wrote, "so vivid and mysterious, was enough to occupy his entire being." *** [referring to Albert Camus' last book-manuscript, found next to his body at the accident scene. [in... and inspired by... Robert Saretzky's study of Albert Camus "]

Mortality. Death.
Humanity's ultimate solidarity.

The bitter, intellectualized foretaste.
Floating... even, amid the pleasures... the plentifulness:
of life and living.

While... the artist:
Impulsively. Furtively.
... the artist...
looks into the bottomless, thirsty eyes,
of the object "de ses désires".

-A sadomasochistic glance at the clock-
A glance encompassing all the "Elements of life." ***

A pause, in this...
the quasi-divine ability, of humans, for self-perception.

Some sort of evolutionary short circuitry:
Imposed... Inflicted on homo-sapiens and their descendants:
In some ironic, galactic lottery.

This precious, exquisite awareness of life.
And its opposite...
in a ditch.

MoMa's unsurpervised project.

Refik Anadol ["Unsupervised"** at the MoMA.]

Paraphrase from the internet site: "... visionary exploration of fantasy, hallucination... irrationality.... alternate understanding of art-making itself." And excerpts of Jean-Yves Solinga, very early (teen age) poem. ["Iced Grass and Lost Youth"] [in "Clair-obscur of the soul"] on the topic of a lovelorn couple, on 'frozen grass' ...looking up at a post-teenage-dance, winter sky.

[*** 'J-Y.S' poem about the "beauty" of the night stars [all freewheeling inert matter of no particular 'beauty' if it were not for human eyes looking at it.

.... Just...
Crystals of water
Giving snow cover,
To wind swept hills:
For nothing
Were it not for man's reflection
On countless explosions.
Bursts of light
Taking metaphoric flight.
Though nature will follow its course
Without man as its source
An empty forest
Is only sterile rest......

[post-script of poem: "There is nothing inherently beautiful about the Universe."

** *New York's Moma computer-generated project.*

Exodus from the past ***

Immigrants, looking at World War Two family pictures... and an alternate life... had the one... 'stopped' in the photograph... not been changed by an exodus to America.

"Oh!?... the man next to my sister... was the neighbor...
We never saw each other, after 'D. Day.'"

Thus, such complex reflections upon...
Human self-determination and illusions, about free-will...

...permeated his university lectures:
... nuanced descriptions...
of wartimes... choices and survivals.

————

Heady days, of strong doses of existentialist heroes
On universities campuses and French-directors, movies.

Like many... post dark ages of societies... and man-made cataclysms
Delusions about humans self-directed improvements.

The ghosts of Candide and Voltaire
were still around.

We were far from...
"The best of best worlds possible."***
And seemingly, ever-close to fatal, ethical wrong choices.

————

The sisters were looking at
-a black and white picture-
-of a gray world-

The baby-face picture: of a collaborating,
-families-murdering-
... traitor of the region.

-Looking at her (pre-war) intended fiancé!-

Moment... safely stopped in time.
Before the whole family's...
exodus for America.

Encapsulated, in this brittle photograph,
Exists... still... a morality tale
A warning of how thin is the varnish
Between civilized humanity
And abject moral darkness.

It happened to 'two souls'
Whose dips into the worlds had lived under the protective glance
Of la Bonne Mère.*****

**** *Protective religious statue overlooking Marseille.*

*** *Scribbled lecture-notes, accompanying this poem and a former one in "Clair Obscur of the Soul" ['Silence of the soul']... a fictionalized inspiration of two men... emotional survivors of World War Two's destructive effects on the ethics of their souls.*

Compilation: based on a fictionalized situation, related to the writer.

Unsupervised

On this....
'the third Rock from its sun'.

Since, the 'natural' beauty of nature's attractions
is unconcerned by humanity's glance upon it.

And because, it is the result of some gigantic chaos theory:
.... MoMa is in line with the concept of
the 'accidental beauty' ... in its vast holdings:

-from various hearth bound Geneses-
-Divine or otherwise-

———

In an absurdist world,

*Survival of the fittest... and human ethics***

"The evidence of this struggle is right here!
Sticking beyond the impeccable white of your cotton shirt or skirt:

Remnants of your body hair:
On your face or legs.

-Or the ever-present need for deodorant!-

-For both genders!"
In response to the smirks.

———

But... it was his anger:
The primordial instinctive reaction.
The mocking laughter.

Towards the awkward...
... bespeckled high school 'nerd'.

Small stature. Shyness with speech.
His awkward, halting expression:
in a new language.
...
"The weakling of the herd!" ...
Wasn't he !?"
... he added.

** Educator, taunting his impeccable retinue of students. Today's topic of the seminar: "Human evolution". Question: what does the 'idea' that YOU... in this... civilized... College-Prep. Environment: are the product of this 'survival'?

Living in a Scene, From a Truffaut Movie

Living in a scene, from a Truffaut movie.
Paris. Orly airport.
At the "Only Passengers" sign.
It was over.

Things could not hold. Or restart.
She knew it. He felt it.

Like all his Genesis-moments:
He became cut-off, from his surroundings.
From all the terminal's steel and glass.

Except for...
the galactically-deep... warm blackness of her glance.
That last instant: that sinners, in love, remember.

It happened, upon entering his own secular, earthly garden.
Just before, gladly giving away his soul:
to that lurking, dark-figure.

The script had yet to be finalized:
Susceptible to all and any changes.

At the mercy of the fickle-humor,
of the director's godlike-whims.

The scenario, not yet written.
Human needs: rekindling the past:
To experience the panoply of being alive again.

——

His only protection:
his words.
He had to... say something insightful.
Deep.
He felt, as if, she expected it from him.

———

He had gone over several drafts.
Beautiful, lyrical sinuosity of sentences.

And yet... all he could say:
as he crumpled the note in his pocket.

As she kissed him: starting to turn around.

Having kept an uncharacteristic silence:
He exploded with:

"I will never fall in love in the same way"…
... He added...
"I think, I know... now,
what lovers mean by these words:

-some loves... some lovers-
Unforcedly... Oh! So naturally!
Refashion your heart, for only their image."

Inspired by re-reading a poem [decades later] referring to that specific scene.

Fahrenheit 451 poem

Peace and war issues...

Decided. Influenced:
Like so much preference in dishwashing pods.

Like a return, to the thumb-up or down decision,
of some Roman, arena circus:

———————

Someone's uncle, not coming home for supper:
Literarily life and death issues...
... Masquerading as sports.

All in the machinery, of a bored audience.

A process, not much better
In some of our presidential discourses.

"I voted for the other candidate":
"I liked their** eyes."

** *non-binary terminology.*

In the "Fahrenheit 451" movie, interactive TV scene, we have a foretaste of the potential lack of proportionality, of individual opinion, built into mass-communication (i.e., the infamous political surveys): the aggressively intrusive, nationwide interview (in her kitchen) of the Julie Christie character: clueless citizenry, opining and possibly dumbing down civic knowledge [the Francois Truffaut 1966 adaptation, of Ray Bradbury's book]

Reconstructing:
New York, at night, on the FDR Drive.

Traffic had been stopped:
Middle of the night.
On one of the buzziest arteries of the city.

And nothing!
Nothing: but reflections into the crystalline winter-night.

Eerie radio silence... for once.

He lowers his window:
Instinctively, looking around, the deserted highway.

Nothing. Nothing...
... but the sinuous lines of the Brooklyn Bridge, across the water.
Prudishly, hiding its towers.

And these words from "New York" by Lépold Senghor:

"New York ! je dis New York, laisse affluer le sang noir dans ton sang
Qu'il dérouille tes articulations d'acier, comme une huilè de vie
Qu'il donne à tes ponts la courbe des croupes et la souplesse des lianes."

"New York! I say New York, let black blood flow into your blood.
Let it wash the rust from your steel joints, like an oil of life
Let it give your bridges the curve of hips and supple vines."***

"So... my English teacher, had a point"...
he whispered, in the cold harbor-breeze.

** The voice of the character, is a fictionalized compilation. A potential drop-out, 'at risk student'... who was introduced to the beauty of poetry and Senghor in a post-graduation, enrichment-night-class.

*** English version: by "Poetry atlas" all right reserved.[not the author's]

"If I ever lose my faith in you." (Sting)

Miniscule hotel room.
Back street: Within the celestial decoupage, in the evening sky,
of the Notre-Dame towers.

Quartier Saint-Germain-des-Prés.
He had done, what he had been reflexively, taught to do...
Pray.
Look up... and pray.
But... there remained only... a tired and cheap candelabra.

———

Having lost any semblance of beliefs
-beyond the useful-rational-
Such as:
the... quasi 'miraculous' Ribonucleic acid of his profession.
Life!
As we know it.
The very consciousness of consciousness itself:
found in the hidden folds evolution...
... among the encrusted, cosmological residues, of our star-dust-Earth.

———

Already... a religious orphan:
He had... therefore, anointed himself,
the high-priest of a self-sufficient orthodoxy.

He had kept...
an apparently indestructible faith in science and progress.
Reserving, for his pleasure(s),
the consciousness... the irrational consciousness:
of the carnal-solidity of her glance.

Poetic delusions.

Arm-chair...satisfaction.
The esthetical.
These beautiful words and ideas...

... chased into their last refuge of human organic awareness...
... last neurological impulses
of his research.

The philosopher/poet... in limitless darkness.
No absolutes possible.
Limitless darkness!

For that philosopher:
-Beyond Camus, et al...

That philosopher...
had... now... to answer:
"If I ever lost faith in you."

With only cotton sheets:
Protecting them from reality.

Sting [the protagonist is a semi-fictional composite]

Losing one's God and Muse

** *"If I ever lose my faith in you."*

Miniscule hotel room... back street:
Within the celestial, découpage of the Notre Dame towers.
Quartier Saint-Germain-des-Prés:
He had done, what he had been reflexively, taught to do...
Pray.
Look up... and pray.
But... there remained only... a tired and lonely... cheap candelabra.

———

Having lost any semblance of beliefs
-beyond the useful-rational-
Such as, the... quasi 'miraculous'
Ribonucleic acid of his profession.
Life!
As we know it.
And the very consciousness of itself:
found by the smart evolution that we have become.

Evolution, found, hiding:
in the encrusted cosmological residues, of our star-dust-Earth.

———

He had... therefore, anointed himself:
the high priest of a self-sufficient orthodoxy.

He had, indeed,
acquired an apparently indestructible faith in science and progress.
But had, however, reserved, for his pleasure,
the consciousness... the irrational consciousness
of the carnal solidity of her glance:

His poetic exemplar, of the iindestructibility of thought.

It had become the safe passage,
for his thought through time and through space!

Poetic delusions.
And the arm-chair, satisfaction of esthetically beautiful ideas:
To their last neurological impulse.
Thought:
And her...THEIR impervious images ...
On their respective soul:
Of a quaint, miraculous, medieval, renewable, unsoiled status!
"If I ever lose my faith in you".
The philosopher in him:
Living fearlessly in limitless darkness.
No absolutes possible.
A limitless darkness'.

-That philosopher-
Beyond Camus, et al ...
-That philosopher-
had... now... the answer...
Reality had been no match to the warmth under the sheets.

*"If I ever lost** my faith in you" ** Out of respect for my second language (English): the subjunctive 'lost' is preferable to Sting's original 'lose'.*

**** Fictionally inspired and written to the looped YouTube of the song.*

***** Source: Musixmatch Songwriters: Gordon Matthew Sumner.*

Read to the looped replay of "If I Ever Lose My Faith" lyrics © Songs Of Universal Inc.

Humanization of an animal behavior

With, as immediate background... (but of course, not only)... the article 'troubling trend in teenage sex' [New York Times, April 12, 2024]

Intellectualization is in our nature:
"Humanity can actually... anticipate the act"!**

Would our hominoid grand-parents, have considered
Gradations... any gradation...
'improper sexual behavior'
in the smoky corners of the grotto?

These grand-parents...
stressing about the deepest intent of the cycles of rut?

Perplexing status of our ribonucleic double-nature:
Chemical evolution producing... self-consciousness.... quasi-miraculous
synapses!

Godlike synapses floating in filthy organic juices!

Thus, the contradictory literary entries in our human vocabulary:
From the lyrical construct of the quasi-religious:
Love.
Untouchable object of desire;
Unsatiated amorous hero.
The medieval love-rondeau...

And yet... in the same book...
Human behavior of hellish, hallucinations:
"Battle-front, rape-centers
of our past and present,

** *Sarcastic comment, from academic, on the other side of the seminar table: "And yet, we work with some of the brightest youth in the nation"... concerning the animal-house behavior from a dormitory,*

Ode to the library shelves.

Writing...
words... thoughts... ideas...
conceptualized realities,
emanating from organic descendants of primordial enzymes:
all and any of these visions,
reproduced by hominoids' smart use of their communicative skills.

To a nihilistic artist the quality of the language
does not make it cosmologically important...
but it should place humans
of on some platform that need to be processed in the viewer's mind
[in the beginning of the artificial intelligence age]

is acquiring the aura of the defiance of early humanity,
giving multi-dimensional meaning to the grotto rock:
time and space
have to yield to the viewer's awareness of their realities.

That is what has been happening in libraries,

"Thoughts": on the quaint art of... WRITING. Or whatever other human... communicative medium [or encephalic neuro-transmission] it will adopt in the far future.

Naked in Paradise

At the asymptotic limit: where artificial intelligence (almost) meets artistic talent.
The symbolic couple is still... symbolically naked in Paradise.

The innovations in 'representing' humanity...
are now, rather done through the eye...
The dead eye...
of an omnipresent iPhone:
———

as faithful... and as capable...
-as all and any-
Renaissance painter.
———

But, unlike the Renaissance painter:
the iPhone, is not a sentient entity.
———

Adam and Eve...
are still leaving paradise in tears...

-but for the A.I. codes-
-in the instrument-
The liquid on their reddish cheeks, is only a bodily function.

And not... the shorthand version...
Of divine condemnation.
———

The visceral stigmata on the couple's souls,
is better felt by the sleep-deprived, visiting tourist.

-Through this reciprocal, knowing glance
-of each... in the guilty couple-

The moral tragedy:
captured and interpreted by the application
of varying hue of layers of paint.

The fibrillations of the brushstrokes.

But especially... especially... the good will of the human viewer
-Toward the artistic piece-
-And the eternity of its intent-

The poet, turning his computer on.

The poet turning his computer on, only to find...
-added verses-
... put in, by the 'machine'.

A hopeful and possibly dark fable.
A tale,
of the still shimmering after-birth of 'Artificial Intelligence'

———

An unprompted, forward leap of a computer program:
Having added on its own, lyrical lines to the piece.

The artist, having diligently been working,
in a world of metaphors... similes.

Childhood and university memories:
Now 'self-encoded into 'verbal-flesh'.

The poet...
at his lonely, late-night ritual:
had turned off the 'machine'.

Not out of depletion of imagery.
But rather exhaustion.

Reciting to himself and his crazed Springer Spaniel
-asleep on his feet! -
The Credo of sentient life:

"I love knowing life and knowing myself living it."
"Our pasts will survive... through this human solidarity."

At the intersection of cultures and civilizations

The painful vestigial surges of feelings**:
Like the phantom pains, of an amputated arm.

The body follows the daily habits.
As though the motion,
could magically turn the pain into flesh!

The most sacred witness to their sensual intimacies:
The sacred temple their bedroom, now a source of tortured
illusions...
... sleepwalking through memories.

A black and white, cinema-verité film.
Quasi-existentialist, Sartrian, stage-drama:

Human beings, condemned to eternally relive their past.
In an empty present.

** *The moribund relationship of a couple.*

Lyrical reaction, of cultural insensitivity [the purpose of the publicity and its upbeat tempo... versus the extreme sadness of the original] resulting from cultural dominance. Claude Francois' (1967) song: "Comme d'habitude".

"Jouer à faire semblant" *

Painful vestigial surges of feelings:
Like the phantom pains, of an amputated arm.

The body follows the daily habits.
As though the daily motions,
could magically turn the pain into flesh!

The most sacred witness to their sensual intimacies:
The sacred temple their bedroom...
now a source of tortured illusions.

Sleepwalks through memories.

A black and white, cinema-verité film.
Quasi-existentialist...
... dead universe of Jean Paul Sartre's stage-drama:
"No Exit".

Human beings, condemned to eternally relive their past.
In an empty present.

"Jouer à faire semblant" is taken from the original French lyrics of "Comme d'habitude" (by Claude François). It literally means: 'Playing... at 'making believe'. The French lyrics express the hauntingly, realistic, moribund, emotional relationship, of a couple. [1967 "Comme d'habitude"]. And not the chirpy, well-intentioned, American commercial adaptation.

The cow and me

Analogous to the biting into the sea salt taste:
On sweet cantaloupe flesh.

The acrid bitterness
Of organized killing...
... laced with...
... moments of our incongruous laughter.

A defanged, mortal enemy:
at attention for the parading cow.

Accompanied by the milk can carrying, escaping prisoner!

———

The pathos of Greek tragedies, is indeed, born of a knowing
... and cooperating, human glance.

The viewer's presence feels, at times, intrusive.
There is an unspoken intimacy.

Marguerite-the-Cow and the French soldier,
seemingly communicating in their special language.

Salty tears... added to the melon.

Inspired by a reviewing of a film, I had first seen, at its release, in Morocco, with my parents. "La vache et le prisonnier" ["The cow and me"].

**More likely a fiction, the story had a real-life consequence on the 'coactrice' [Marguerite-the-cow]. The animal had been destined for the 'abattoir' [slaughterhouse] but the actor Fernandel and movie's director provided for the bovine-star to die of old age, on a farm.*

Heart-wrenching, 1959 French movie, starring 'Fernandel': portraying an escaped French P.O.W. on a German farm, who decides to walk back to France and freedom. All this, through the military controls... while 'guiding' the farm animal.

That young German soldier

Very little room for geo-politics, in a mother's mind.
Or for quantum theories of space and time, of academia.

She had to be in two places at one time:
And "she would be"!

The harsh realities of wartime unforgiving violence.
The all-encompassing dimension of maternal love.

Or answering the questioning confusion
-in grade-school children-
being pulled on their arm.
...
No amount of soothing 'dolce voce' encouragements
Made those little legs go any faster.

And thus, the solidity of war
met its eternal nemesis:

A battle between...
The limpid-blue eyes of a mother
and its effect on a trigger finger. **

** *The hesitation and refusal to shoot, on the part of the German sentinel:
considered by the author an existentialist engagement of the future... since he
would not have existed, had his mother been killed.*

Based, on real events: [World War 2 Marseille: the author could no longer confirm the family folklore that Allies were bombing the port]. It is the confrontation of a 'young' German soldier, stopping a mother of two grade school children (attending two different establishments). They are stopped for being in the streets, after siren-warnings, to clear the streets [another woman has already been wounded].

[To the looped playing of Marvin Gaye's "Mercy Mercy Me".]

In danger of falling in love

Could it be, that Hollywood,
in the celluloid plasticity of its beliefs...
-and by some happenstance-
... had included the proper human representation
of fear ...***
... in the eyes... the great, blue-green eyes,
of Charlton Heston, as Moses:
looking at his God?

Is this the same unverbalized apprehension.
-recognized despite its subtility-
for other human's experiences, in privileged moments?

The same, out-of-body feeling, in the confine of a 66 VW:
becoming limitless, through the awkwardness of a teenage kiss.

That...
what you are whispering to each other
will somehow become real...
... by the simple humid passion and innocence of the moment.

That the mandates, of societal and familial constraints,
appear to have been waived by the jealous gods:
looking down on this couple.

———

As Claude Lelouch had wisely advised the actors:
to simply be... "a man and a woman." ***

This affirmative command:
coming down on the movie-set.

Hinting at a cosmic exception, granted to lovers.

———

But!... what a spectacular remark about human truths!

To have distinguished the most ephemeral and sacred
illogical... ...non-codable feeling...
of human fear!

Fear, of lovers, haplessly gazing
at an opening chasm
of their multiplying futures.

———

Falling in love:
The absorption: of all one's present and all one's future,
into her glance!

———

And then, reading this commentary,
in the fickle and slick world of a publicity...
... Leaving him... decades later...
-back in that infinitesimal space, in a miniscule car-

Listening for echoes of tremors of his rite of passage:
Bouncing off the Watch Hill lighthouse.
In the fertile, late-summer, nuptial darkness.

*** *"What is very mysterious and very interesting about the way Claude Lelouch portrays that connection and that love story is that you can feel the danger of it. They are already falling deeply in love with each other." [Commentary (in NYT) by Penelope Cruz, about the characters of "Un homme et une femme". She was on a publicity campaign, as Ambasssadrice de la Maison Chanel] [with some punctuation editing (jys)]*

Chills of New England

Under his boots...
the chill... the chills of his new home.
The chills of New England.

Frozen cement stairs... from frozen street.

And yet,
Somehow, no conflicts in his accommodating heart.

All this...
Despite the solid layer of frost
on the inside of the family kitchen.

———

No surprise. Just simple adult abdication.
For he still had,
on the warm side of his hallucinations:
in the yard...
the grayish, dead summer grass.

Safely home now...
to sleepy vipers and scorpions.

-Layered emotional realities of gardens-

The Monet of his current books!

But… then why…
the burning of tears?

New immigrant, studying in his overheated dorm-room.

"From poetry... to computer programs" **

"From poetry to computer programs."
Innocuous article headline.

Touting the deserving accolades
of potential for pharmaceutical discoveries:

The exponential capacities:
from the old fashion, refrigerator, tray-sized experiments...
... to the nano physics.
Of multi-million studies at once!

———

Parents of sick children
Reading these words, through tears!

———

But what of the trivialization! **
The scientific arrogance of including
the sacred... vaporous...visceral:

Human-generated poetry!

Would we want to read the 'appetizing' headline:

"Three-star Michelin restaurant, letting the in-house A.I.,
make its famous Coq-au-vin:

-Rich clair-obscur of the sauce-
-Shades of Rembrandt's dark browns-
-Layers of réductions-

And no-one!
No human, having tasted the sauce, a priori!

Except. Maybe.
A simple, light-spectrograph,
of the chicken, in its bath?

** *From an article [N.Y.T. June 17, 2024]. Overly optimistic capabilities [by adding poetry] about the co-founders of Terray' {a generative A.I.} and its use in pharmaceutical research.*

An invincible Summer

"In the depth of winter, I finally learned that there was in me an invincible summer." (Albert Camus)**

There must exist,
privileged souls.

Descendants of an era that precedes the gods.
The gods... and their commandments.

Autonomous beings. Free.
Without aims. Orders or dimensions.
The few happy people... clear of mind.
Without innate fears. Without taboos. Forethoughts. Or Pretenses.

Having taken the measure
of their part of responsibility.

Itself...
imposed by the meaning of their rank:
Which is,
that of humans... within humanity.

Mankind,
therefore, sensing and taking account of this weight.
This realization.

———

That... the stellar dust
-Our mother-
Is not guilty, for the injustices of this world.

———

But rather, that the formers are not... never had...
-nor will ever have-
another source, than us.

Inspired by one of my rereadings [and audio] of Albert Camus' acceptance speech of his Nobel Prize.

** The 'solar world' of Albert Camus' youth [and me], plays a big part in my thesis of the Maghreban landscape. [University of Connecticut]

Fear of existentialist engagement.

« Je me suis toujours demandé ce qui leur était arrivé » ...   ["I had often wondered what had happened to them."

Bittersweet and unexpected meeting, in an academic symposium, of former university roommates: one of whom had introduced his friend to "the love of his life". [circa middle 1970's]

"Ok! Ladies and gentlemen:
Our next topic:
'Existentialist engagement'*
....
Those words, of their philosophy professor, came to his mind:
-His roommate was in love! -

The blind date...
...had been a spectacular success!...
...
... but an atheist, himself:
he felt, a guilty unease, at 'playing-at-deities'.

———

It was, later,
over a cordial cup, of awful symposium-coffee,
that he learned
of the catastrophic, heartbreaking details...
of unreciprocated love.

———

The true nature of their friendship was sealed
all these years latter
accompanied by humid glances on both sides:

"No... no... don't apologize:
your action... gave me a lifetime of human lyricism!
Looking into her bottomless dark eyes!
Merci... mon ami!

* A confession made to another class: "That's why I was reluctant to get involved with 'fixing' dates': I had underlined that section from Jean-Paul Sartre."

"Let me introduce myself" *

Very late night... and very heady, university 'bull-session'.
Topics:
... getting increasingly phantasmagoric:
in proportion to the opacity of fumes, in the tiny dormitory quarters.

———

How... fate...
... imposes tragic ends, to beautifully, talented humans.

———

Tonight's tragic figure:

The setting and actor:
A James Dean persona...
Looking into his bathroom mirror.
An attractive male figure, appears in the foreground:

A disincarnated voice is heard:

"You will die… young!
Never having known... the pain
-by simply looking at yourself-
-In a future mirror-

... the passage of time!"

———

Comment, from someone
on cluttered bed:

"In retrospect,
there was a shooting-star aura about them."

"After the announcement of their death...
It somehow, sounded like an inevitable classical tragic ending!"

"The gods, building these superhumans... perfects figures!
Living in finely chiseled, sandcastles turrets.
With their finely chiseled souls."

"And... these waves all around!"

————

"I saw a certain sadness in their glance,
A poetic, canary friability, in their energy.
As though, they KNEW... of their brevity in time."

"Seemingly... already longing for what they had seen in the mirror."

* Fictional reconstruction (with poetic license) of visit(s) from a persona, à la Rolling Stones' "Their Satanic Majesties Request". The all-powerful figure, giving the artist a glance, and choice, into their future: such as meteoritic fame: but early death. [Jim Morrison, Jimi Hendrix, Prince.

Dream sequence 2: Hitting Bottom✶✶

Writing. When there is nothing driving the activity.
Writing. When the personal muse is long gone.

When the object of desire has become, mere black points.
-White and blue, screen-flatness. of Microsoft-

_____

This is, when the essence of feelings,
is cooked up in the bowels of a personal hell.

You find yourself, scrapping the dry residues of yesterday.
You lick them:
like some block of salt, in front of a thirsty cow,
back from the pasture.

What an image!
She... the goddess of your world...
has become akin to this white, dry powder, that bites into your tongue.

_____

And then…. a sharp sensation!
It transports you.
You put down the glass of 'crémant de chardonnay'.
To, then listen to the bubbling inside of you.

This dried up essence of HER glance
is the most potent and precious worldly thing that you have ever felt.

Now. All is over.
No remaining reason to write:

But rather accept another social invitation
-To mimic happiness-

-Anything: but putting another thought on paper-

————

And then... and yet. Uncontrollably.
A quasi-masochistic wave washes over your mind.

Like a classical culinary réduction.
The best of a bouillon:
reduced to its most essential ingredients.

The sort of intensity of taste that goes beyond the moment.
-It had stayed in your soul. All these years! -

It enters your memory bank. The kind of taste that you can reconstruct:
At will. Later. On your palate.

** Inspired by its original version.

From "Pages from a personal Mythology"

It's all in her glance *

** Einstein 'E=mc2': meets the Muse of Alfred de Musset of "Nuit de mai".

[Voice of the muse]
"Poet, take up your lute and kiss me
The eglantier's flower feels its buds emerge:
Spring was born tonight; the winds come to embrace it
And the shepherd girl, waiting for dawn
Perches on the first green bushes
Poet, take up your lute and kiss me."
[excerpts from: "May night" by Alfred de Musset.]

[La voix de la muse]
Poète, prends ton luth, et me donne un baiser;
La fleur de l'églantier sent ses bourgeons éclore.
Le printemps naît ce soir; les vents vont s'embrasser ;
Et la bergeronnette, en attendant l'aurore,
Aux premiers buissons verts commence à se poser.
Poète, prends ton luth, et me donne un baiser.

It had been there all the time!
Our very own genesis.
Our creations. Our creation!
Gentle photons of sweetness,
emanating from our corner, of the cosmos!

———

Everything... that would be anything...

... had been there:
at its infancy.
In miniscule... insignificance.

But everything!!!
It had never made much sense:
Until... Until...the moment, when I realized

that all these sighs...
... all these whispers
... had, always been there.
My presence. My senses...
...gave human meaning...
... to what ... otherwise, would have been lost.
In the inert solidity of things.

———

The artist... confronting his art:
... realizing, that he had been living among HER.

* Poem triggered by the poet, having mindlessly, mechanically... gone through his decades of notes: stored in boxes.

** With that four-letter equation, Einstein, famously spoke...mathematically... if not poetically... as he entered the world of his reality. With a basic fact that: the amount of energy, produced by a certain quantity of mass, is equal to that mass: multiplied by the resulting number of the speed of light... multiplied by itself. While, Alfred de Musset begins his opus-entry into his artistic world, hand in hand, in a sensual dialog with a vaporous Muse.

A Bee in Monet's Garden
A fable

To the looped music of Paul Hardcastle [Northern Lights]

"Artists and their art, are often sensitive intermediaries*** between the inert solidity of the Cosmos... and human, sentient-awareness of life and living." [concluding remarks in professor's notes on a lecture on Charles Baudelaire's 'Correspondances']".

He woke up... full of pollen.
Reflecting on his trajectory among things,
He considered himself...
-his whole life-
to have been, one of a pollen-intoxicated bee.

One of Stendhal's happy few:
that had wandered into precious moments of happiness.

Those youthful moments, of the natural, tactile... immediacies of living.

Yet... full of contradictions.
Such as the eternity of glances:
-her glance-

And their heartbreaking opposites.

———

But, unlike that bee,
his human self-introspection:
the need to express his passion of living
made it possible to recreate! .....

-like all artists and lovers-

….. Such memories as the sensual intoxication
of the cool Sahel-ocean mist off of Sidi Moussa.****
over their teenage bodies.

———

While, all along, outside of the paradisiac flower-garden,
existed the inescapable… absence of these very desired and desirable
objects.

———

Thus… it happened, as these things often do…
-In the middle of floating black butterflies-
… covered with the yellow, fertile mucus and parfum
of future flowers…
… that he remembered his classroom comment,
regarding doomed extermination-camp prisoners,
that…
"dying in such hopelessness in front of one's eyes",
was the biggest insult
to the cosmological miracle of consciousness-of-life.

———

And so, his gods
[crying marble-tears]
granted his wish.

———

Having suffered a massive heart attack.

Managing to sign himself out of the American Hospital of Paris.

With a smile and just a simple tear…
he died.
….

With the birdlike-shouts of children, playing,
at the nearby Place des Vosges.
Surrounded by the self-dilutional solidity of man-made monuments.
The immediacy and flashes of moments of whispered-hedonism:
under wavy cotton sheets.

-His mind running through pieces of the universe-

From deep in his inert soul
-In an ultimate collective act-

Leaving the future to everyone.
And everything else to others.

———————

And then…
… this surprising, noble gesture from a dumb and deaf universe.
A parting gift.

SHE seemed to be still there!

Her milky, cottony-translucence,
in the window frame.

A "Clair-Obscur of his Soul":
Silhouetted against Montmartre,
in the background.

Biting into his last taste
of disincarnated… infinitesimal eternity.

And yes
[and probably]
as blind luck would have it:
a last sparkle of a Maghreban little beach: **

in an otherwise disinterested…
Time and Space.

[Inspired in part by the author's reaction to the Léon Monet exhibition, at the Musée du Luxembourg: "Ah! To have been a bee… in Monet's garden!!"]

** From "Bled and snow" [unpublished memoirs]

*** Correspondances "by Charles Baudelaire".

La Nature est un temple où de vivants piliers
Laissent parfois sortir de confuses paroles;
L'homme y passe à travers des forêts de symboles
Qui l'observent avec des regards familiers….
Nature is a temple in which living pillars
Sometimes give voice to confused words;
Man passes there through forests of symbols
Which look at him with understanding eyes.["Les fleurs du mal" Charles Baudelaire.]

**** "Sidi Moussa" [unpublished memoirs]

Between computer-coded reality and artistic dreams

A futuristic view of art and the artist

Between coded and organic realities: exist dreams
-of a humanity-
generating wispy thoughts and aspirations.

As well as nightmares from humans, stringing beads of sweat,
made of folds of flesh.

Our earthy bestial appetites:
Having artfully, extracted from our surroundings.

———

WE... sentient organisms
-issued from the cooled-off crust of stardust-
Describing our home.

-Humanity's self-awareness-
Of the slime that has slithered-out, from the opened paradisiac gates.

———

It all began with the prehistoric dreams.
in grotto-colored mud and on grotto walls.

-Reconstructions of life and living-

Captured and controlled by humans.
-For humans. For their pleasure-

The artist:
Often the intermediary

between:
-Reality and passion-

Translated into pieces of realism.
By billions of bites.

Between Sidi Moussa and Napatree* Point

Human lyricism... in its ethereal, vaporous universe:
can violate...
... its own laws... of an envious universe.

Allowing us to revisit:
a pre-paradisiac innocence.

Allowing: the precious 'happy few'...
to relive their very passion of moments.

Their sighs... smells... and frissons:
Previous seconds... and thus, years!

The humanist miracle of seeing yourself!
In that car:
... discerning Block Island, through its vibrating lights.

-Decades later-
-In time and space-
-Space and time-

"Je t'aime... tu sais!"

Knowing that we will cry:
for having, only temporarily, been granted to hear,
those precious words!

Blood-red, precious lips.
Jealous gods.

"Je t'aime... tu sais!"

Napatree point: an emotionally, 'sacred' sandbar, across from Watch Hill, in Westerly, Rhode Island. In the early seventies, it was a perfect place, of benign neglect and relative quiet, for "reliving [in his early adulthood-years: in his new culture and new job] ... in an apparent, bottomless world of 'earthy' and 'heartly' happiness. The very sensual exaltation, as the one he had known, on the salt-eaten rocks of the Barbary-coast: within sight of that 'other 'sacred site': the mausoleum to Sidi Moussa [the prophet Moses], in Salé, Morocco.

The Artist, Inspiration and Time [Reprise]
Napatree Point, Watch Hill.

"His words were forming a translucent lace.
A clever netting where the spaces and knottings
Were magically linked.
Only his art could give birth to such filigree." ***

————

Cosmological gamble... taken by a young poet.
The above words... not chiseled in bluish,
Grecian marble...
But in the acrid ardor, of still-pulsating flesh.

Emanations of her Grasse, floral-parfum
burning his lungs, with every breath.

Now as in the past:
The wager is won!!

The moment... the gaze...
... All had survived in the folds of time:

Redeemable... in the unexplainable dimensions, of time and space.

Lyrical hiding places... reserved for the "happy few".

Those,
who instinctively, set aside extracts of the sur-abondance
of the happiness of youth.

To be spread on the wrinkled lips of age:
Like a hedonistic... blasphemic... pre-religious...
Humanistic:
extreme unction.

*** ["The Instant of the last glance" Chapter 5 – Voices. From "Clair-obscur of the soul"]

Cosmic 'Reverse-engineering' ***

We will have reversed
Untold eons of evolutions

-dead ends... and miraculous solutions-

Walking, the Earth on bare feet:
Followed by space travel.

The so called... mineral dumbness of things:
Versus...

[In the eyes of the exquisite beauty
of the crying beauty
of a violin solo.]

-The arrogant predominance
Of mind over matter-

———

Humanity's unstoppable arch, toward the keys to everything:
Nothing resisting...
... the inquisition of smart mathematical equation.

Even the atom... now... having infinitesimal particles!

-Humanity and its descendants
Will have climbed back up
That lonely and bear Sinai mountain-

Finding, a hidden and cowardly god,
made of eternal black.

Humanity will have come back from that Sinai mount, with tears in its eyes and full of an orphaned sadness: having learned that the only answer, is the hands of the person in the mirror.

*** We will eventually have learned enough, to know that the answer [and a modicum of happiness] will have indeed been like, the momentary happiness of Camus' Meursault, on that sunny Maghreban beach.

Electric-blue eyes

Assignment for first-year instructor: going from desk to desk to match "the person" with the name on printout. [late sixties: pre computer ... pre-everything, years].

"She had electric-blue eyes"!
He wrote in his ambitious, notebook, that night:
... "as she looked up from her desk"...

"Miss**... what is your last name?" ...

-In this multi-language... multi-cultural setting-

He never did... remember...
which language, she had used, to answer.

———

It reminded him, of one these scenes... of a special-forces soldier...
-Dropped on foreign soil-
... with the next seconds: determining his future!
......
Everything else, in the room.
had become simple, stage props.

It must have been the tongue of prophets.
The one... used by 'illuminated souls'...
... who converse with bushes!

A quasi-divine communication skill
Handed down, at times, to humanity:
from the lyrical side:

to compensate for the loss of paradise.

Along with... eternal damnation...
... short-cut for the "happy few" ****
Between the sleepy mundane and happiness.

————

-The attendance taken-
... he had... ever since, tried to retaste....
the miraculous, unexpected nature, of the next seconds:
which is the essence of all cherished moments.
...
He never did... have the occasion or courage...
to approach the 'student'... behind the glance.

His youth and timidity
had made her untouchable...
... and she was gone.

** *Contingent of foreign students, in 'immersion' classes, for their first-year American-college studies.*

**** *Unknown to the instructor: her student-visa would have issues and eventually be retracted. ["Happy few" ... Marie-Henri Beyle's [Stendhal] favorite expression for being in love.*

*Artist... in a malleable*** universe*

He was the one,****
The silent-one... who kept himself away from the others.

Always, a little late from hunting :
For having wanted more time
in order to look at a sunset.

Or more time...
... to spot the source
of a particularly pleasing bird-song.

The one, who
-returning with food-
on a beautiful summer day...

... offered a river-smooth, blueish talisman-stone,
to the mother of his child.

**** *Speculation, on the first hints, of 'lyrical escape', from this bizarre member of a prehistoric, (hominoid) tribe. The one, who liked to coat his index, with ash-coal... and trace on the cave walls, images that formed in his mind.*

*** *[malleability of the artistic universe] of their world [reality] : "... reality is at times, no more than play-dough ! ... to be fashioned or refashioned at the will of the human mind." [unattributed comment, from the 'Martell Cognac-corner, of the room]*

L'artiste dans un univers malléable. ***

C'était lui…
Le silencieux… qui se tenait souvent un peu à part.

Toujours un peu en retard de la chasse :
Pour avoir voulu, plus longtemps observer, un beau coucher de soleil.

Ou bien chercher du regard
… la source particulièrement, plaisante d'un cri d'oiseau.

Celui qui… un beau jour d'été… revenant des champs avec la nourriture :
Offrit une belle pierre-talisman, aux reflets bleuâtres,
à la mère de son enfant.

Spéculation sur les premiers moments d'évasion lyrique de l'humanité hominoïde ; chez ce membre un peu 'bizarre' d'une tribu préhistorique, qui aimait enduire son index de cendre de bois… et former sur les murs de la grotte, des images qu'il voyait dans son esprit.

*** Le terme « malléable » ici, utilisé par un membre d'un groupe d'académistes à la retraite, discutant la vision des fois imposée par les artistes sur la réalité : « … pour certains d'entre eux, le monde [la réalité] n'est que de la pâte à modeler.

A soul with no topography

He had never adjusted
to the promiscuity of the imposed friendships
of university-dormitory life.
Thus, keeping a personal reserve, in his social temperament.

So... the surprising ease,
of his friendship with this "fine arts" major.

This floor-mate. A budding artist. A smiling demeanor.
Limpid, blue eyes. Muscular physique!
Somehow, not clashing with his declared major:
Fine arts!

But an unusual combination, making for easy week-end dating.
Too easy: for his low emotional quotient.
The unforced simplicity of personal conquests.
Not much inhabiting in his universe!
A freshman: with the attraction... of an attractive, empty vessel.

Even his Grand tour of Europe,
narcissistically associated with the femininity of museum paintings.
And his mental "little black book"!

Had there ever been any human febrility:
between the brush and his canvases?

Reflections on the place of Artificial Intelligence-created art and its role in the "INTENT" behind the work. This author remembering, the mechanically gorgeous paintings of this particularly talented artist, with no pathos.

Pastis near the Kasbah

Drinking, Paul Ricard Pastis, in New England heatwave.

It was the gentle surprise…
The unexpected… antithetical feeling with the setting….
A place
usually associated with winter-backyard, Siberian ice.

Now… with no personal effort…
An emotional transport to hypnotic Maghreban music
from the Kasbah across the street.

My early tastes of Pastis from my father's glass!
Rite of passage…
worth his sly smile of approval.

All that past…
all those presences and things that define us.

All of it and more…
as soon as the acrid-sweetness hit my lips…
-in now-
my "New-World".

The solidity of the past

La reconstruction de Notre Dame de Paris.

Engineer-in charge (Villeneuve)..." I said (upon hearing about the fire)... that the little boy who was in love with the cathedral and the architect in charge of the cathedral... died that night and another man took over."

[Paraphrase of television program(s) on Notre Dame de Paris]... Burly member of a small army of workers, using purposefully, centuries-old, woodcutting tools, in a low, emotional voice, explaining, his purpose: "This is such an honor, to be working on this project... these trees... individually chosen... their ultimate purpose... to rebuilt exactly like our medieval predecessors."

There was an over-arching,
surprising sense of sotto voce...
an intimacy in the comments:
in an otherwise semi-industrial setting... of cranes and scaffoldings.

A seemingly, natural relationship between complete strangers.
Extraordinary, quasi-sensual,
reincarnation
of "the" medieval carpenter who worked on
this particular portion of this huge beam:
again... almost whispering:
"you can feel, how he fashioned this piece...
the slight indentation into the grain...
... from centuries ago!"

Making that tree trunk
Sound like a Madonna marble.

———

This state of mind... of quasi-symbiotic energy:
flesh...and monument

recurring against the background-setting:
the Hugoesque grandeur
of a still-living building.

————

An Italian, art-school student…
-running her fingers over the damaged stones-
… and YET adding…

"You can feel, why he did not completely square this stone"…
… "it is costume-cut to stabilize this section".

"We have to repeat the imperfection…
to make this physical contact, last again, for centuries."

————

Not simply… subserviently rebuilding:
but rather… and somehow… embodying the mason and his glance.

The "soft skin" of huge, milky stones from the original quarries,**
handled with surgical dexterity!
"We'll do it… with our heart… passion… and knowledge":
from…a bespectacled, structural engineer… rebuilding the spire:

"IT" will be a magical moment!"
… a surviving, sculpted-rose, in his hands.

————

Apparently filling the cavernous-voids:
a chaotic, metallic-lace of tubing…
… in the midst of left-overs of carnage and demolition…

A sort of secular "rebirth" …
… heard in the "confessional-tone" of television interviews:
one hundred feet, over the romance of Paris.

** *Most of the original limestone, for Notre Dame de Paris, came from the underground of the fifth and twelfth arrondissements of the city.*

Pilots in a transatlantic flight to Paris

Philosophy in the cockpit of an Airbus **

[Second Officer]] "Landing in zero visibility, with only our equipment to guide us, could be compared to A.I. taking over the destiny of sentient-life on Earth ... but in our case... the human pilots can at least take over the controls... and play the role of the gods."
[First Officer] "If you're comparing this cockpit to humankind and earth... and since, I'm a card-carrying non-believer... our next minutes, are... and will be determined by the quality of the software and my flying ability."

After the flight: reflecting at his favorite terrasse, on rue des Martyrs.

The adage:
"There are no atheists in foxholes"
... came to his mind.
It still evoked intellectual disdain, after all these years!

As a fledging, expat-artist in a 1960's Paris.
An already, fully formed existentialist.

A card-carrying absurdist...
... knowing that Godot would not show up.

He fully believed in Camus' human solidarity:
That... the only lifeline is...
"This scared, other twenty-year old, in the foxhole, with you."

———

As an artist and writer:
he decided to believe only in the deities that he had painted or created.

———

To him, sentient or non-sentient life
... was simply the result of cosmological luck.

And humanity's self-awareness
… was the source of anguish
… Not… fear of death,
but rather, the resulting fear of losing the awareness
of the deep throbs of HAPINESS!

———

Ah! … Opportunistic hedonism:
For simply being alive!

But fear, of these envious, mythological gods!

-Envious of human happiness-

The ones, described by the character in Henry Miller's Paris:
Fear of a jealous person coming in the room
and interrupting things…
between himself and two women. ***

———

So, for the first officer [and our humanity]
it was the number of miles, before landing safely in Paris, that mattered:

Thinking to himself:
"A.I. can help me land this thing…
but it will not… wax lyrical… change its codes…
… in order to internalize her glance."

All this metaphysics at 30,000 ft!
leading to languorous reciprocal, Claude Lelouch-glances, on each other…
neo-classical façades
and breakfast with HER!

** *Going to Paris and… a breakfast [grand crème, croissant et tartine beurrée]
at Place Saint Georges, rue des Martyrs.*

*** *"Paris Genesis" Jean-Yves Vincent Solinga.*

To the continuous replay of Hardcastle's "Northern Lights".

Unexpected human kindness...
in military barracks

1960's, Viet Nam War era, boot camp. ***

It must have been his even-handed,
blank look...
to the incomprehensible additions
to his new world.

As immigrant... silence was safer:
in shouted directives.

Innovative, new lexis of insults
from drill sergeants...
left him expressionless.

Yelling... with the extra syllables
of Southern accent, did not help:

It was simply ...
A New World, in his New World.

———

His small feet, almost sending him home:
All the boots were too big.

Exhibiting the empty firing chamber of his M-16
Leading to an exasperated:
"Private!...
... how many years of High School do you have?
_ Four years of college... sergeant"

———

From fellow draftee on K.P.**
"What did you do wrong: to be on K.P."?
_ "Volunteered... I like to cook"!

———————

But all that unforced helplessness
had ironically, softened the heart of the terror-of-the-squad:

A huge, scary loner:
his designated, bunkmate:

"You're not White... you're French... you're OK!"......
....
... was the awkwardly, fraternal support, he would need...
until graduation.

1960's, U.S. Army boot-camp, of mostly drafted, Viet Nam-bound soldiers. One of them, from a European-country, puts him (somehow) in a "non-white category by a very muscular and very "angry" black, fellow-bunk mate. Circumstances led to an improbable friendship.

***** Fused compilations of events.*

**** K.P. [Kitchen duty], sometimes used as punishment.*

Aborted dreamscapes of youth

*[This poem is my love letter to the Maghreb of my childhood]

The sensuous setting of his youth:
A place of deadly, Bled vipers, hiding in the afternoon heat.

Always in French... 'pantalons-courts':
Exposing his upper legs...

-And having accidently squatted in spiny-quasi-desert grass-
-Playing desert-explorer-

The sharp needles of arid plants, scrapped his thighs.

-A quasi-explosion of orgasmic, electric sensuality! -
Activating his pubescent confusion-

———

A direct... unbroken, envious link into his adulthood.
Strange gravitational attraction:
Of the other worlds... of the New World.

Time and spaces:
fabricated
from sharp-edged realities and lyrical whims.

Having found ... an up-to-then unknown kinship
with other 'created worlds':

-The Singing detective... a literary, long-lost cousin!-

The dangerous nuptials, of realities to dreams:
that would reappear in future 'Proustian' recurrences.

———

Freezing, February nights:
On dangerous, New England roads.

The heat of the Sahel
Strangely fogging
The jealous, back-window of the '64 Volkswagen!

———

All these sensations of hedonistic paradise, filling his soul
... as the ball-bearing...
made a direct hit on his temple...**

From personal-notebook pages [for contemplated biographical-fiction]

*** The narrator, having been hit on a raised, thick-winter collar... would have to soon, leave [unscathed] the land of his youth.*

Albert Camus, better known in the English-language as a philosopher [the Absurd and Nihilism] wrote in loving, expansive (lyrical) prose about Algeria: the land of His birth. See "La femme adultère" (in, "L'exil et le royaume") ... one of the best poetic intersections of human sentient-life and the nothingness of the desert!].

Inspired by marginal notes for bio-fictional work: "Sidi Moussa: We lose the youth; but keep the passion." [Jean-Yves Vincent Ciccariello Solinga] (In U.S. Copyright Office, unpublished division) and chapter of Albert Camus, in chapter 3 [Albert Camus] "Evolution et constantes..." University of Connecticut Dissertation (in French) Jean-Yves Solinga,

Jean-Yves Solinga in Paris

Jean-Yves Solinga, Poet

Jean-Yves' poetry is one of cultural duality. His poetry draws you into a world of intellectual contrasts: where one reality is juxtaposed with another. Creating a multi-dimensional universe that is all at once: simultaneous, fascinating, unsettling and revelatory.

He is a poet with an effortless ability to use language: conveying a multitude of emotions. Thus, resulting in an ambiance of subtlety and immense depth. His free-prose style of poetry [lyrical prose] is not in the least affected or pretentious. He has an expansive historical vision, linked to the narrative voice of a poet.

His poetry makes one relive through some of the important social and intellectual upheavals of the past: all this, through words that reach the depths of the soul. His poetry tries to redefine the capacity of poetry-itself. Poetry as it could be. As it should be. The art of expressing pure thought about the existential human condition. His books contain many breathtakingly, beautiful and sophisticated poems, that reach out to the very limits of that human condition, where true art exists. The body of his poetry is a product of... and symbolically reflects... a life of cultural duality and a search for an artistic resolution with the past.

Raised in the "solar" heat and light of Morocco, he migrated to the "Labradorean" cold coastal waters and countryside of New England. His father, mother, sister and brother had gone through the tragic, second world-war years of 'allies' bombings and Nazi occupation in Marseille: that feed tragic moments in his poems.

Born in the Sidi Bel Abbès, on the periphery of the Sahara in Algeria, the vast empty space of the desert haunts his imagery. His parents regularly went to Sidi Moussa, a mausoleum (to the prophet Moses) near Salé, in Morocco: one of the poles of his life and writings. The pleasure of sight and exotism of his childhood landscape, became a major part of his dissertation.

Living in New England, introduced him to snow. Thus experiencing, firsthand, one of his many future encounters with freezing cold and snow, while up to that time he had seen that universe only in Christmas cards. Noteworthily, it became the impetus for one of his first teenage poem.

The title "Clair-obscur of the Soul", of his first published book, is indicative of this cultural duality, and is a recurrent theme in many of his poems. His... is a world of intellectual contrasts, and juxtaposed cultures. Accompanied with a constant study and awareness of being (at times) the "Other". As you read Jean-Yves' poems, you witness a poet with an effortless ability [and notable pride] who uses an organically born language and metaphors of emotions, without recourse to the artificial intelligence of computer codes.

Jean-Yves' poetic-prose style is not affected or pretentious; but rather innate... natural: a perfect mate to his expansive vision and voice, as a poet. He often revisits the fundamental issue and concept of "reality" in the creative and emotional drive of the writer. He makes use of fragments of the day-to-day mundane life: whereby, a French corkscrew can become a link between two souls and two cultures. Imaginative attenuation, between things real and imagined are often microscopically thin but never broken entirely in his writing.

He again, explores humanity's perception of reality as an existentialist, in the absurdity of things and people. All the time, seamlessly mixing between beauty and unspeakable horror. Space and time. Time and space. He imagines inimitable, multilayered, multifaceted poetic images that bring the reader both nearer to uncomfortable truths [in which most would not willingly venture] or to a point of passion or beauty that we could not have previously envisioned.

While most writers wait for the muse to appear or reveal itself to them, to Jean-Yves, every memory, event, spoken word, or visual stimulation has significance and potential: requiring an immediate response. Nothing in his stream of consciousness or... in fact, unconsciousness, is irrelevant to the process of creating his poetry.

Jean-Yves embraces the world with clear-eyed enthusiasm. There is a kind of joy in these poems, tempered by hard-edged vision. The 'virile' nature of a feminine voice. The capture of a whole culture by the by the hypnotic repetition of a drum. The gesture of planting a tree in the mud of a yard. The rubbing of fingertips on the left tower of Notre Dame de Paris. All find their natural place within his lines. Jean-Yves casts a cold eye on the past and uses it in a prism to reconstruct its place in a present.

He manages to unravel complex knots of situations without destroying its parts: Helping us understand how they're woven. He uses grammar to transform speech. Transform lives. Hopefully, refashioning the future. This is what poets do and poetry does. And all done, with the delicacy and beauty, of indeed, interwoven Majorelle-Blue silk lace.

Jean-Yves is at ease with the cultures of museums: as well as the intricacies of a meal. He celebrates the workers as well as the cathedrals: seeing traces of lyricism left behind by both. And especially, especially... he values each moment... seeing eternity. Not the hour; but the single second... into the glance from the object desire.

Other Books by Jean-Yves Solinga

Clair-obscur de l'âme

Clair-Obscur of the Soul

In the Shade of a Flower

Landscape of Envies

Words Made of Silk

Impressions of Reality

Artist in a Pixelated World

Asymptotes at the Infinity of Passion

Created Reality

Paris: Genesis of a Muse

Rage and Passion

Black Butterfly Dust

www.ingramcontent.com/pod-product-compliance
Lightning Source LLC
Chambersburg PA
CBHW081003140626

46546CB00018B/3179